Exploring Data

Revised Edition

Exploring Data was originally prepared under
the auspices of the American Statistical
Association–National Council of Teachers of
Mathematics Joint Committee on the Curriculum
in Statistics and Probability.

This book is part of the Quantitative Literacy
Project, which was funded in part by the
National Science Foundation.

Exploring Data

James M. Landwehr
AT&T Bell Laboratories
Murray Hill, New Jersey

Ann E. Watkins
California State University, Northridge
Northridge, California

DALE SEYMOUR PUBLICATIONS

This book is published by Dale Seymour Publications, an imprint of the Alternative Publishing Group of Addison-Wesley Publishing Company.

This publication was originally prepared as part of the American Statistical Association Project—Quantitative Literacy—with partial support of the National Science Foundation Grant No. DPE-8317656. Any opinions, findings, conclusions, or recommendations expressed in this publication are those of the authors and do not necessarily reflect the views of the National Science Foundation.

Order Number DS21143
ISBN 0-86651-610-7

6 7 8 9-ML-98 97

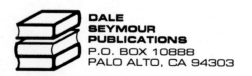

DALE
SEYMOUR
PUBLICATIONS
P.O. BOX 10888
PALO ALTO, CA 94303

CONTENTS

PREFACE

Exploring Data, now revised to include current data sets and a completely new section on dot plots, is an introduction to statistics. In addition to learning the most up-to-date statistical techniques, you will have an opportunity to practice techniques in other areas of mathematics.

Familiar statistical topics, such as tables of data, the mean (average), and scatter plots, are included in this book. Less familiar topics, such as the median, stem-and-leaf plots, box plots, smoothing, and dot plots, are also included. All these techniques are part of an emphasis in statistics called *data analysis.* Data analysis de-emphasizes the use of algebraic formulas for analyzing data. Instead, data analysis stresses the importance of organizing and displaying data so that it reveals its patterns and surprises. The techniques of data analysis are easy to use and are frequently graphical.

John W. Tukey, an influential statistician now retired from Princeton University and AT&T Bell Laboratories, was the leader in this new approach to statistics. He first published some of these techniques in the 1960s and 1970s. Rarely in your study of mathematics will you learn methods developed so recently.

The techniques in this material encourage you to ask questions about data. This is an important part of data analysis. By using these methods you will be able to interpret data that are interesting and important to you.

––––––––––

The authors gratefully acknowledge the inspiration and leadership of Jim Swift in the preparation of materials on data analysis for secondary students.

I. NUMBER LINE PLOTS

The table below gives the attendance, in millions, at the top ten amusement parks in the United States in 1993.

Park	Attendance in Millions	Park	Attendance in Millions
Walt Disney World, FL	30.0	Sea World, CA	4.0
Disneyland, CA	11.4	Knott's Berry Farm, CA	3.7
Universal Studios, FL	7.4	Cedar Point, OH	3.6
Universal Studios, CA	5.0	Six Flags Great Adventure, NJ	3.5
Sea World, FL	4.5	Busch Gardens, FL	3.5

Source: *Los Angeles Times*, May 23, 1994.

Let's make a *number line plot* of these data. Put a scale of numbers below a line. Since the smallest attendance is 3.5 and the largest is 30.0, the scale might run from 0 to 35 as shown below.

```
┌┬┬┬┬┬┬┬┬┬┬┬┬┬┬┬┬┬┬┬┬┬┬┬┬┬┬┬┬┬┬┬┬┬┬┐
0       5       10      15      20      25      30      35
```

The attendance for the first amusement park, Walt Disney World, is 30.0. To represent this park, put an X above the line at the number 30.

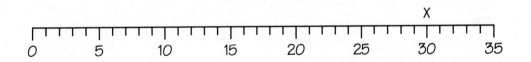

Continuing this way with the other amusement parks, the completed number line plot is shown as follows. Each number has been rounded to the nearest million so the X's don't look crowded.

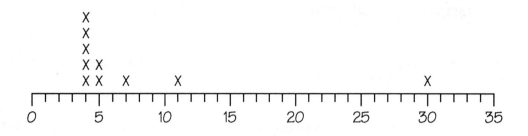

From a number line plot, features of the data become apparent that were not as apparent from the list. These features include:

- *Outliers*—data values that are substantially larger or smaller than the other values
- *Clusters*—isolated groups of points
- *Gaps*—large spaces between points

It is also easy to spot the largest and smallest values from a number line plot. If you see a cluster, try to decide if its members have anything special in common.

Discussion Questions

(Discussion questions are meant to be done either by the class or in groups.)

1. Make an estimate of the amount of money a typical person would spend at Walt Disney World. How much money do you estimate Walt Disney World took in in 1993?

2. The population of the United States is about 260 million. What percentage of the U.S. population went to Disneyland or Walt Disney World in 1993? What assumptions must you make to do this calculation?

3. Often we would like to know the location of a particular point of interest. Invent a way to show that the X at 30 on the number line plot represents Walt Disney World.

4. Why is there a cluster at 4 and 5 million? What would the plot look like if it included the top 25 amusement parks?

5. In this book, you will often be asked to "describe what you learned from looking at the plot." Try to do this now with the number line plot, then read the following sample.

The number line plot shows the 1993 attendance, in millions, for the top ten amusement parks in the United States.

Two features of the plot stand out. One is that on the number line plot, the seven parks with the smallest attendance are clustered at the low values, between 3.5 and 5 million. This is what we would expect because the attendance for only the top ten parks is given. If more parks were included, we would expect the number line plot to have a large number of X's between 0 and 3 million. It would be interesting to see this plot.

The second feature that stands out on the plot is that the largest value, for Walt Disney World, is an outlier. With attendance of 30 million, Walt Disney World has about three times the attendance of the next highest park, Disneyland. The number of visitors to Walt Disney World is about the same as the entire population of California, the most populous state.

It is interesting that the top six amusement parks are Disney (Florida and California), then Universal Studios (Florida and California), and then Sea World (Florida and California). All but two of the top ten are located in Florida or California, states where people go for vacations.

Writing descriptions is probably new to you. Think first about what the data measure and how they could have been collected. If you have comments or questions about where the data came from or what they measure, include these comments in your description. When you look at the plot, jot down any observations you make and any questions that occur to you. Look specifically for outliers, clusters, and the other features. Then organize and write your paragraphs as if you were composing them for your English teacher. The ability to organize, summarize, and communicate numerical information is a necessary skill in many occupations, and it is similar to your work with science projects and science laboratory reports.

Application 1

Soft Drink Sales

The table below gives the major soft drink brands with the percentage of total soft drink sales in food stores. For example, Diet Dr. Pepper accounts for only 0.9% of the total soft drink sales in food stores.

Soft Drink Brand	Percentage of Soft Drink Sales in Food Stores
Regular Pepsi	16.1%
Diet Pepsi	5.7
Slice	1.6
Mountain Dew	3.2
Regular Sprite	2.6
Diet Coke	7.4
Coca-Cola Classic	15.9
Regular 7Up	2.9
Diet 7Up	1.2
Regular Dr. Pepper	3.3
Diet Dr. Pepper	0.9
A&W Root Beer	1.2

Source: *Beverage World Magazine*, 1992.

1. What percentage of food store sales is held by brands not listed? What are some of these brands?

2. About 6,100.2 million gallons of soft drinks are sold annually in food stores in the United States. How many gallons of Coca-Cola Classic are sold in food stores?

3. Food store sales account for about 50% of all soft drink sales. How many gallons of soft drinks are sold annually in the United States from all sources, including food stores?

4. Coca-Cola Classic is the largest-selling soft drink if we count all sources of sales. From all sources, about 2351.1 million gallons of Coca-Cola Classic are sold in the United States annually. What percentage of the total market is held by Coca-Cola Classic? Why is this percentage higher than that listed in the table above?

5. The population of the United States is about 260,000,000. On the average, how many gallons of Coca-Cola Classic does an American consume annually? This is the equivalent of how many 12-ounce cans?

6. Make a number line plot of these data. First round each percentage to the nearest whole percentage.

7. Write a description of what you learned from looking at the number line plot. Discuss any outliers, clusters, or gaps.

4

8. (For soft drink experts) The soft drinks are listed in the same order they were listed in *Beverage World*. Is there any rationale for this order?

Application 2

Chronic Conditions in Young Americans

The National Center for Health Statistics issues tables giving the prevalence of chronic health conditions in the United States. These are broken down by age group; the table below is for people under the age of 18 and gives the rate per 1000. As an example, a rate of 1.4 for arthritis means that out of 1,000 people in the United States under the age of 18, we can expect that 1.4 of them will have arthritis.

Condition	Rate Per 1000 Under the Age of 18
Arthritis	1.4
Asthma	61.0
Bladder disorders	3.1
Chronic bronchitis	50.5
Chronic sinusitis	68.9
Deformity or orthopedic impairment	29.3
Dermatitis	35.7
Diabetes	1.8
Frequent constipation	8.2
Frequent indigestion	1.9
Hay Fever without asthma	59.7
Heart disease	17.1
Hearing impairment	15.6
Hernia of abdominal cavity	4.1
High blood pressure	2.2
Kidney trouble	1.8
Migraine	15.5
Tinnitus	1.7
Trouble with corns and callouses	0.2
Trouble with dry skin	9.9
Trouble with ingrown nails	9.1
Ulcer	0.9
Visual impairments	9.0

Source: National Center for Health Statistics.

1. Of 1,000 people under the age of 18, how many would you expect to be hearing impaired?

2. Of 1,000,000 people under the age of 18, how many would you expect to be hearing impaired?

3. Suppose there are 200,000 people and 300 have a certain chronic condition. What is the rate per 1,000 people?

4. Of 2,500 people under the age of 18, how many would you expect to have heart disease?

5. Construct a number line plot of these data. To avoid crowding when plotting the X's, round each rate to the nearest whole number.

6. Write a summary of the information communicated by the number line plot. Include a list of any questions you have about the data.

Possible project: Select one of the chronic conditions listed above. Write a letter to your U.S. senator or representative making the case that the U.S. Congress should allot more money toward finding a treatment or cure for this condition. You may want to investigate whether there are effective treatments now and whether research is currently adequately funded.

Number Line Plots — Summary

Number line plots are a quick, simple way to organize data. They work best when there are fewer than 25 numbers. With many more, the plot starts to look crowded.

From a number line plot it is easy to spot the largest and smallest values, outliers, clusters, and gaps in the data. It is also possible to find the relative position of particular points of interest. Sometimes you can notice outliers, clusters, and gaps from the table of data. However, the number line plot is easy to make and has several advantages. It makes it easy to spot these features, it gives a graphical picture of the relative sizes of the numbers, and it helps you make sure you aren't missing any important information.

When making number line plots, be sure to place the X's for values that are approximately the same on top of each other rather than crowding them in. It is also usual to number the scale in multiples of 1, 5, 10, 100, or some other round number.

Suggestions for Student Projects

1. Collect data on one of the ideas listed below or on your own topic. Make a number line plot of the data and write a summary of the information displayed by the plot.

    - heights of students in your class

    - grades on the last test for the members of your class

    - ages of the mothers of students in your class

    - number of hours of television you watch each day for two weeks

    - number of miles each student drives in a week

    - number of students in your class born in each of the 12 months (On the number line, 1 would represent January, 2 would represent February, and so forth.)

    - number of raisins in each student's small box

2. Is there any relationship between the percentage in Application 1 and the amount of shelf space given to the soft drink in your local supermarket?

3. The incidence of asthma among the young has been rising in the United States. Investigate reasons for this rising rate.

II. DOT PLOTS

Many people think that astrology—the belief that the positions of heavenly bodies affect the destiny of people on the earth—has some sort of scientific basis. The table below gives the percentage of adults in various "developed" countries who said astrology is either "very scientific" or "sort of scientific." The number surveyed was approximately 1,000 in each country.

Country	Percentage	Country	Percentage
Belgium	51%	Ireland	52%
Canada	45	Italy	46
Denmark	61	Luxembourg	62
France	61	Netherlands	57
Germany	54	Portugal	48
Great Britain	54	Spain	64
Greece	53	United States	35

Source: National Science Board, *Science and Engineering Indicators*, 1991.

If someone looked at just a number line plot of these data, they would not be able to tell where a given country was located. The plot we will make in this section, called a *dot plot*, can be used in the same situations as number line plots, but it includes the labels for each data point.

To make a dot plot, first put the data in order from largest to smallest. The countries above would appear in the following order.

Spain	64
Luxembourg	62
Denmark	61
France	61
Netherlands	57
Great Britain	54
Germany	54
Greece	53
Ireland	52
Belgium	51
Portugal	48
Italy	46
Canada	45
United States	35

Next, make a number line on the top and on the bottom of a box. Our scale goes from 0% to 70%. We might have chosen 0% to 100% if we had wanted to emphasize what part each percentage is of the whole population. List the countries to the left of the box. Finally, draw a light line from each country

9

across the box until it is under the country's number. At that point, draw a heavy dot.

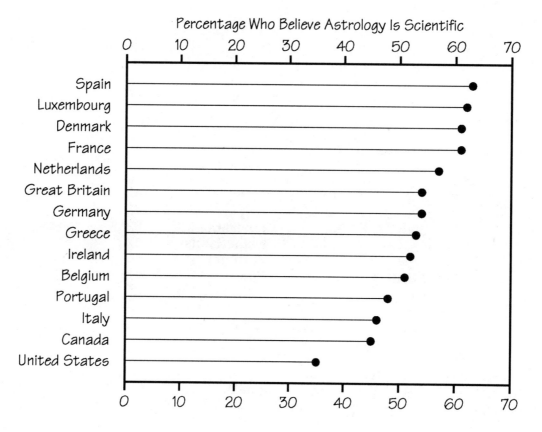

For a second example, the *Los Angeles Times* recently listed the 15 most popular names of the more than 200,000 licensed dogs in Los Angeles.

Name	Number of Licensed Dogs
Lady	2,214
Max	2,055
Rocky	1,471
Brandy	1,363
Bear	1,338
Blackie	1,321
Lucky	1,293
Princess	1,283
Duke	1,216
Ginger	1,156
Pepper	1,014
Sandy	838
Sam	799
Samantha	786
Shadow	777

Source: *Los Angeles Times.*

Here is a dot plot of these data.

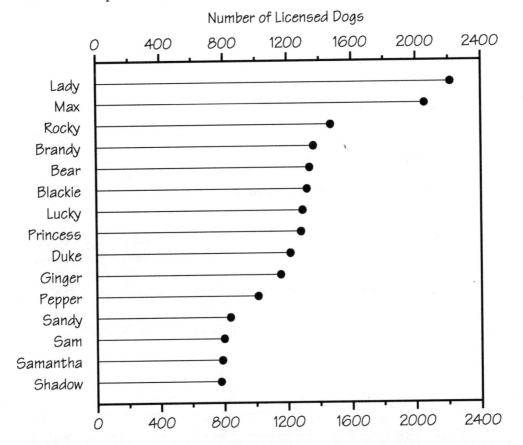

A second type of dot plot should be drawn in cases where it is awkward or not helpful to include 0 on the number line. For example, the following table gives the proficiency scores of 13-year-olds on the mathematics section of the last International Assessment of Educational Progress.

Country	Average Math Score
Canada	513
France	519
Hungary	529
Ireland	509
Israel	517
Italy	517
Jordan	458
Korea	542
Scotland	511
Slovenia	504
Soviet Union (Russian speaking)	533
Spain	495
Switzerland	539
Taiwan	545
United States	494

Source: National Center for Education Statistics, *The Condition of Education,* 1993.

Here is a dot plot of these data with a scale that extends from 0 to 600.

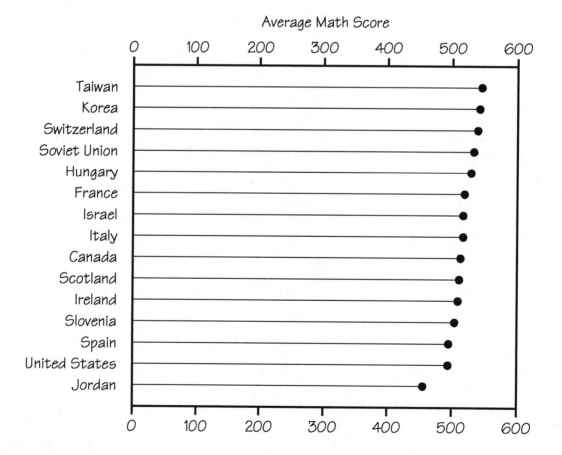

This dot plot makes it difficult to see whether there is any difference in the scores from country to country. Here is another dot plot with a scale that extends from 450 to 550.

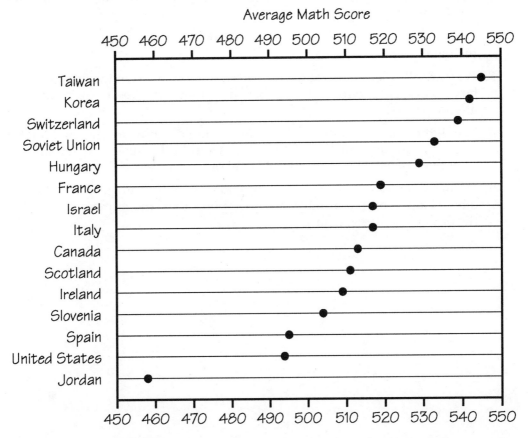

Average Math Score

Notice that the light lines go all of the way across the box. If the lines went just to the heavy dots, as they do in the plots beginning at 0, a person who looks at the plot would be tempted to compare the relative lengths of the lines. For example, a line from 450 to 545 for Taiwan would be more than 11 times as long as a line from 450 to 458 for Jordan. In fact, Taiwan's score isn't 11 times as great as Jordan's. We don't want the person looking at the plot to compare lengths so we draw the light line for each country all the way across the box.

Discussion Questions

1. Give a situation where a dot plot would be better than a number line plot for displaying the data.

2. Give a situation where a number line plot would be better for displaying the data.

3. Why are all labels and tick marks for the number lines on the outside of the box? (Compare with the number line plot for the amusement park attendance data.)

4. The light line goes all of the way across the box in the plot of the international mathematics scores. Why would it be misleading to stop the light line at the heavy dot and not go all of the way across?

5. Make a dot plot of the data on the attendance at amusement parks. Should 0 be included on the number line? Do you prefer the number line plot or the dot plot for these data?

Application 3

Problems in Public Schools

The Gallup poll gave adults in the United States a list of more than 30 issues concerning public schools. The poll asked the adults which issues they thought were a problem in the public schools. The percentages are shown on the dot plot below. The ten items listed are all of those that had 5% or more of the respondents think the issue was a problem.

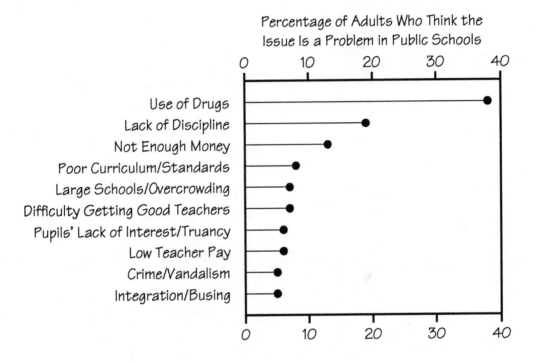

Source: *Phi Delta Kappan*, September, 1990.

1. Is there any issue that a majority of adults think is a problem in the public schools?

2. What percentage of adults think that crime/vandalism is a problem in the public schools?

3. A Gallup poll typically surveys around 2,000 people. About how many people in the poll said that large schools/overcrowding is a problem?

4. Do these data suggest that adults are relatively happy or unhappy with the public schools? Explain.

5. Do you think adults would answer differently today than they did in 1990?

In another survey at about the same time, eighth-grade students were asked about problems in their school. The following table gives the percentage of eighth-grade students in public schools who consider the problem listed to be a serious problem.

Problem	Percentage of Eighth-Grade Students Who Consider It a Serious Problem
Student tardiness	12.9%
Student absenteeism	12.9
Cutting class	16.1
Robbery or theft	14.1
Student possession of weapons	11.8
Vandalism of school property	15.2
Physical conflicts among students	17.8
Physical abuse of teachers	7.9
Verbal abuse of teachers	11.9

Source: National Center for Education Statistics, Schools and Staffing Survey.

6. Make two dot plots of these data, one where the scale starts at 0 and one where the scale starts at 7.0. Which do you prefer?

7. Write a paragraph about what you have learned about perceptions of problems in the public schools.

Application 4

Best-Selling Magazines

The table below gives the average number of copies sold per issue of the best-selling magazines in the United States that are written for young people.

Magazine	Copies Sold
Seventeen	1,915,426
YM	1,340,415
Boys' Life	1,288,545
Mademoiselle	1,219,159
Sesame Street	1,218,722
Rolling Stone	1,211,586
Teen	1,188,257
Scouting	1,030,194
Car and Driver	1,019,630
Elle	901,619
Motor Trend	887,475
Hot Rod	856,774
Sassy	682,000
Edge	200,000
Dirt	150,000

Source: Audit Bureau of Circulations (from *The World Almanac and Book of Facts*, 1994, and *The New York Times*, January 18, 1993).

1. There are about 8,500,000 girls aged 13 through 17 in the United States. About what percentage of them buy *Seventeen*?

2. The best-selling magazine in the United States is *Modern Maturity*, published by the American Association of Retired Persons. Its paid circulation is 22,879,886. Complete this sentence: For every person who buys *Rolling Stone*, there are _____ people who buy *Modern Maturity*.

3. Why are the sales of *Edge* and *Dirt* so much smaller than the others?

4. Make a dot plot of these data. Should the number line start at 0?

5. Write a paragraph about what you have learned about magazine sales. You may want to check the latest edition of *The World Almanac* to get current sales. You can also get sales information inside some issues of your favorite magazine.

Application 5

Consumption of Fresh Fruit

The table below gives the number of pounds of fresh fruit the average person in the United States eats in a year.

Fruit	Pounds per Capita
Bananas	24.6
Apples	21.6
Oranges	12.6
Grapefruit	6.9
Grapes	6.9
Peaches	4.2
Pears	3.4
Strawberries	3.3
Pineapples	2.0
Plums	1.5
Nectarines	1.5
Other citrus	4.9
Other noncitrus	3.4

Source: U.S. Department of Agriculture, *Food Consumption, Prices and Expenditures.*

1. About 260,000,000 people live in the United States. How many pounds of bananas do we eat per year? How many tons is this?

2. About 4,475,000,000 pounds of fresh onions are sold in the United States per year. How many pounds of onions is this per person?

3. Name some "other noncitrus" fruits. Name some "other citrus" fruits.

4. How many pounds of fruit does the average person in the United States eat per year?

5. Make a dot plot to display the data in the table above. Should the number line include 0?

Dot Plots — Summary

Dot plots were invented in 1981 by Bill Cleveland of AT&T Bell Laboratories "to display data in which each value has a label associated with it that we want to show on the graph." Often, bar graphs are used for data that would be better displayed on a dot plot, especially when it is unnecessary, awkward, or irrelevant to include 0 on the number line.

Like number line plots, dot plots work best when there are fewer than 25 numbers. With both plots, it is easy to spot the largest and smallest values and outliers. Spotting clusters and gaps is harder with a dot plot than with a number line plot. However dot plots are more useful if we want to see many labels.

Suggestions for Student Projects

1. Make a dot plot for the data in Application 2. Compare it to your number line plot. Discuss the advantages of each graph.

2. Find an example of bar graphs in the newspaper, in magazines, or in textbooks. Draw dot plots of the same data. Do you prefer bar graphs or dot plots? Give your reasons.

3. The table below gives the percentage of eighth-grade public school *teachers* who consider problems in their school to be serious. Invent a variation of the dot plot to display both these data and the data from the eighth-grade *students* given in Application 3. A person who looks at your plot should be able to compare easily the student percentage and teacher percentage for a given problem.

Problem	Percentage of Eighth-Grade Teachers Who Consider It a Serious Problem
Student tardiness	9.4
Student absenteeism	13.7
Cutting class	4.4
Robbery or theft	2.3
Student possession of weapons	1.7
Vandalism of school property	5.5
Physical conflicts among students	8.0
Physical abuse of teachers	1.5
Verbal abuse of teachers	11.3

Source: National Center for Education Statistics, Schools and Staffing Survey.

4. Devise a method to estimate the number of pounds of grapes you eat in a year. Is multiplying the number of pounds you eat this week by 52 a good method?

5. With your class, design and carry out an experiment to test whether the astrological horoscopes printed in newspapers "work." Here's how one class in San Francisco did it: The teacher had a friend in another city who

subscribed to a newspaper that ran an astrology column different from those available in San Francisco. On, say, Tuesday, the friend phoned the descriptions of the 12 horoscopes to the teacher. On Wednesday, the teacher mixed up the horoscopes and asked members of the class to select the one that most accurately described how their day went yesterday. If the horoscopes don't work, will some of the class still select the horoscope for their astrological sign? What fraction of the class should do this?

III. STEM-AND-LEAF PLOTS

The table below gives the number of calories and grams of fat, carbohydrates (sugar and starch), and protein in each serving of various items sold at Burger King.

	Serving Size (g)	Calories	Protein (g)	Carbo-hydrates (g)	Fat (g)
Whopper	270	570	27	46	31
Whopper with Cheese	294	660	32	48	38
Double Whopper	351	800	46	46	48
Double Whopper with Cheese	375	890	51	48	55
Cheeseburger	115	300	16	28	14
Whopper Jr. with Cheese	145	350	16	30	19
Hamburger	103	260	14	28	10
Whopper Jr.	133	300	14	29	15
Bacon Double Cheeseburger	149	470	30	26	28
Bacon Double Cheeseburger Deluxe	185	530	30	28	33
Double Cheeseburger	161	450	27	29	25
BK Broiler Chicken Sandwich	154	280	20	29	10
Chicken Sandwich	229	620	26	57	32
Ocean Catch Fish Filet Sandwich	165	450	16	33	28
Chicken Tenders (six piece)	90	236	16	14	13
Chef Salad without dressing	273	178	17	7	9
Chunky Chicken Salad without dressing	258	142	20	8	4
Garden Salad without dressing	223	95	6	8	5
Side Salad without dressing	135	25	1	5	0
French Fries (medium, salted)	116	372	5	43	20
Onion Rings	97	339	5	38	19
Apple Pie	127	320	3	45	14
Cherry Pie	128	360	4	55	13
Lemon Pie	92	290	6	49	8
Snickers Ice Cream Bar	57	220	5	20	14

Source: Burger King's *Your Guide to Nutrition.*

Suppose you decide to order a Whopper. It contains 31 grams of fat. How does this compare to the other items? By looking at the table, about all we can see is that it does not have the most fat nor the least. So that we can get a better picture of the grams of fat per serving, let's make a stem-and-leaf plot.

First, find the smallest value and the largest value.

The smallest value is 0 for a side salad and the largest is 55 for the Double Whopper with cheese.

The smallest value, 0, has a 0 in the ten's place and the largest value, 55, has a 5 in the ten's place. Therefore, we choose the *stems* to be the digits from 0 to 5.

Second, write these stems vertically with a line to their right.

```
0
1
2
3
4
5
```

Third, separate each value into a stem and a leaf and put the leaves on the plot to the right of the stem.

For example, the first value in the list is 31, for the Whopper. Its stem is 3 and its leaf is 1. It is placed on the plot as follows:

```
0
1
2
3  1
4
5
```

The second value in the list is 38. Its stem is 3 and its leaf is 8. Now the plot looks like this:

```
0
1
2
3  1 8
4
5
```

Continuing in this way gives the following plot:

```
0  9 4 5 0 8
1  4 9 0 5 0 3 9 4 3 4
2  8 5 8 0
3  1 8 3 2
4  8
5  5
```

Next, on a new plot, arrange the leaves so they are ordered from smallest value to largest. (This final step is often omitted.)

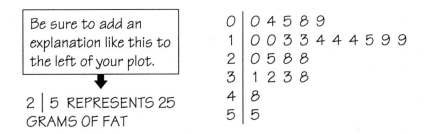

The plot shows that most of the food items have between 0 and 38 grams of fat and that there are two large values. The Whopper with 31 grams has one of the larger amounts of fat.

If we rotate the stem-and-leaf plot 90° counterclockwise, we get a plot that resembles a bar graph or histogram.

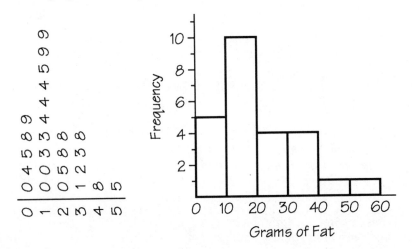

The stem-and-leaf plot is often better than the bar graph or histogram because it is easier to construct and all the original data values are displayed.

It is sometimes worthwhile to label specific items. For example, we might want to label the smallest value, the largest value, and a value of special interest such as the Whopper. This is shown below.

```
0 | 0 4 5 8 9
1 | 0 0 3 3 4 4 4 5 9 9
2 | 0 5 8 8
3 | 1 2 3 8
4 | 8
5 | 5
```

SIDE SALAD WITHOUT DRESSING

WHOPPER®

DOUBLE WHOPPER WITH CHEESE

Also, it is sometimes interesting to replace the leaves in the stem-and-leaf plot with symbols identifying the items. For example, replace each of the eleven hamburger leaves with an *H* each of the three sandwich leaves with an *S* each of the four salad leaves with an *L*, and each of the remaining leaves with an *O* (for other). Replacing the leaves with symbols gives the following:

```
0 │ L L L O L
1 │ H S O O H O O H H O
2 │ O H H S
3 │ H S H H
4 │ H
5 │ H
```

When writing a description of a stem-and-leaf plot, look for the same features you looked for with a number line plot:

- largest and smallest values
- outliers
- clusters
- gaps
- the relative position of any item important to you

Our description of what we learned about fat in the Burger King food items from the stem-and-leaf plots follows:

> *There are no outliers separated far from the rest nor any large internal gaps among these values. Of these fast foods, the type that is generally highest in fat is the hamburger, which has the highest four values. One hamburger is quite low in fat, it is called the "Hamburger." The Hamburger is smaller than the others; only four items weigh less.*
>
> *From the data, the type of food that is second highest in fat is sandwiches; the values are only slightly smaller than those for hamburgers. Again, one sandwich, the BK Broiler, has quite a bit less fat than the other sandwich values and it isn't much smaller than the others. Although we generally think of fish and chicken as having a lot less fat than beef, perhaps the Chicken Sandwich and Fish Filet are fried and are therefore higher in fat.*
>
> *The type of food lowest in fat is the salad, but that may be because salads are given without dressing. The "other" items are spread throughout the lower end of the data; they are a mixed group including fries, pies, and ice cream.*

When analyzing data throughout this book, you will need to examine the plots and to think about other information you may know that can help to interpret the results. Sometimes, this process will lead to questions and possibilities about the problem that cannot be answered from the data alone.

The stem-and-leaf plot shows the shape of the set of data more clearly than a line plot. The "shape" of a set of data is called its *distribution*. Some common types of distribution follow:

Scores on a Test

```
5 | 4
6 | 6 9 9
7 | 2 4 4 5 5 9
8 | 1 1 7
9 | 8
```

Bell - Shaped

Weight in Kilograms of
Children and Their Fathers

```
2 | 5 5 8 9
3 | 2 3 4 4 5 8 9
4 | 0 3 4 5 9
5 | 4
6 | 1 1 3 8
7 | 0 1 3 4 4 5 6 8 8
8 | 2 3 5
9 | 4
```

U - Shaped

Number of Movies Seen in the
Last Year by Each Student

```
0 | 0 1 2 2 2 3 6 8 8 9
1 | 1 1 2 4 4 5 7 7 7
2 | 2 2 3
3 | 7 8
4 | 4
```

J - Shaped

Last Two Digits of the Phone
Numbers of Students

```
0 | 2 3 5 6 6
1 | 0 1 2 5
2 | 0 1 5 9 9
3 | 2 2 3 8
4 | 1 5 7
5 | 0 4 4 9
6 | 1 1 5 7 8 8
7 | 3 6 8 9
8 | 2 4 4 5 8
9 | 0 0 0 3 8
```

Rectangular - Shaped

The bell-shaped distribution is a shape that occurs often. The data values are fairly symmetrical, with lows balancing the highs. If the data follow a U-shaped distribution, it may be because there are really two underlying groups, each of which is bell-shaped, corresponding to the two peaks. Thus, when a U-shaped plot is observed, it is a good idea to see if there is any reason to treat the observations as two separate groups.

The J-shaped plot (or the backward J-shaped plot) does not occur as often as the first two types. Typically, it occurs because it is impossible to have observations above (or below) a particular limit. In the example above, there is a lower limit of 0. If you observe a J-shaped plot, try to determine if there is a limit, what it is, and why it is there. For a rectangular-shaped distribution, sometimes called *flat* or *uniform*, there are often both lower and upper limits with the data values spread evenly between them. For the previous example, the limits are 00 and 99. As with the J-shaped plot, you should try to understand if there are limits to the possible values of the data, and what the limits might mean.

Discussion Questions

1. Make a stem-and-leaf plot of the grams of carbohydrates in the fast food items. Label the smallest value, the largest value, and the Whopper.

2. Make another stem-and-leaf plot of the grams of carbohydrates, but replace the leaves with the symbols:
   H for hamburger
   S for sandwich
   L for salad
   O for other

3. Write a description of the information displayed in the stem-and-leaf plot of the grams of carbohydrates. Mention any interesting patterns. How does this plot compare to the one for fat?

4. All of the fast food information was given on a per item basis. However, the weights of the items are different. Do you think this should be taken into account? How might you do this?

5. In judging fast food items, which is most important to you: calories, fat, carbohydrates, or protein?

6. Would each set of data below be U-shaped, bell-shaped, J-shaped, or rectangular-shaped?

   a. scores on an easy test

   b. heights of the female teachers at your school

   c. heights of all the teachers at your school

   d. percentage of the sky that is cloudy at noon for all days in a year (Check it out!)

   e. number of school days missed in a school year for all students in your school

7. To determine the percentage of calories that come from fat, multiply the number of grams of fat by 9, then divide by the number of calories and, finally, convert to percent. For example, the Whopper has $\frac{31 \times 9}{570} = 0.49 = 49\%$ of its calories coming from fat. Make a stem-and-leaf plot of the percentage of calories that comes from fat for the items from Burger King.

Application 6

Ages of U.S. Presidents at Their Death

The table below lists the presidents of the United States and the ages at which they died.

Washington	67	Filmore	74	Roosevelt	60
Adams	90	Pierce	64	Taft	72
Jefferson	83	Buchanan	77	Wilson	67
Madison	85	Lincoln	56	Harding	57
Monroe	73	Johnson	66	Coolidge	60
Adams	80	Grant	63	Hoover	90
Jackson	78	Hayes	70	Roosevelt	63
Van Buren	79	Garfield	49	Truman	88
Harrison	68	Arthur	57	Eisenhower	78
Tyler	71	Cleveland	71	Kennedy	46
Polk	53	Harrison	67	Johnson	64
Taylor	65	McKinley	58	Nixon	81

1. Make a stem-and-leaf plot of the ages using these stems.

```
4 |
5 |
6 |
7 |
8 |
9 |
```

2. How many presidents died in their forties or fifties?

3. Who lived to be the oldest?

4. Label the four presidents who were assassinated.

5. What is the shape of this distribution?

6. Write a one paragraph description of the information shown in the stem-and-leaf plot; include information about the presidents who were assassinated.

Application 7

Thunderstorms

The table below lists 81 United States cities with the number of days per year with thunderstorms.

Area	Number of Days	Area	Number of Days	Area	Number of Days
Akron, OH	39	Detroit, MI	33	Oklahoma City, OK	51
Albany, NY	28	El Paso, TX	36	Omaha, NE	51
Albuquerque, NM	43	Fargo, ND	30	Orlando, FL	85
Anchorage, AK	1	Fresno, CA	5	Philadelphia, PA	42
Atlanta, GA	50	Grand Rapids, MI	37	Phoenix, AZ	20
Austin, TX	40	Great Falls, MT	27	Pittsburgh, PA	35
Bakersfield, CA	3	Hartford, CT	28	Portland, ME	20
Baltimore, MD	24	Honolulu, HI	7	Portland, OR	7
Baton Rouge, LA	80	Houston, TX	59	Providence, RI	21
Beaumont, TX	63	Indianapolis, IN	47	Raleigh, NC	45
Biloxi, MS	80	Kansas City, MO	50	Richmond, VA	37
Birmingham, AL	65	Las Vegas, NV	13	Rochester, NY	29
Boise, ID	15	Little Rock, AR	56	Sacramento, CA	5
Boston, MA	19	Louisville, KY	52	Salt Lake City, UT	41
Buffalo, NY	30	Los Angeles, CA	6	San Antonio, TX	35
Burlington, VT	27	Manchester, NH	24	San Diego, CA	3
Charleston, SC	58	Memphis, TN	50	San Francisco, CA	2
Charleston, WV	45	Miami, FL	71	Seattle, WA	6
Chicago, IL	36	Milwaukee, WI	37	Shreveport, LA	58
Cincinnati, OH	52	Minneapolis, MN	36	Sioux Falls, SD	47
Cleveland, OH	38	Mobile, AL	86	St. Louis, MO	43
Columbia, SC	52	Nashville, TN	52	Tampa, FL	91
Columbus, OH	36	Nassau-Suffolk, NY	18	Tucson, AZ	28
Corpus Christi, TX	32	Newark, NJ	25	Tulsa, OK	53
Dallas, TX	41	New Orleans, LA	73	Washington, DC	28
Denver, CO	38	New York, NY	18	Wichita, KS	53
Des Moines, IA	55	Norfolk, VA	36	Wilmington, DE	30

Source: U.S. Weather Bureau.

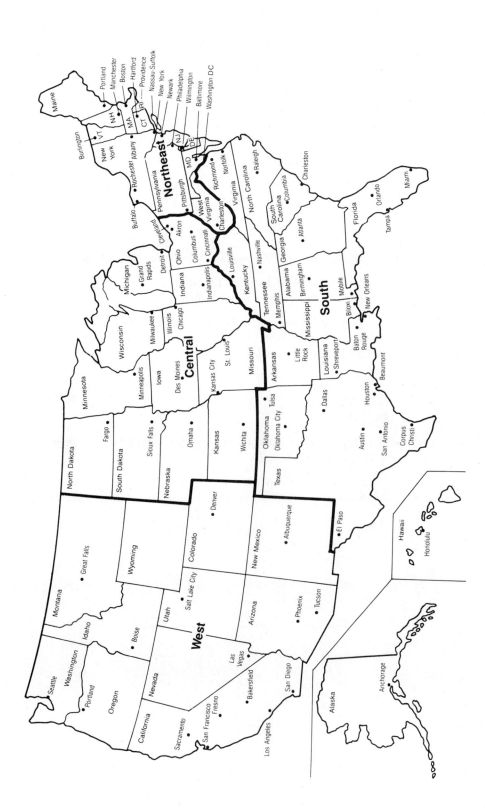

A stem-and-leaf plot of the number of days of thunderstorms is shown below. Notice that the stem for numbers less than 10 is 0.

```
0 | 1 2 3 3 5 5 6 6 7 7
1 | 3 5 8 8 9
2 | 0 0 1 4 4 5 7 7 8 8 8 8 9
3 | 0 0 0 2 3 5 5 6 6 6 6 6 7 7 7 8 8 9
4 | 0 1 1 2 3 3 5 5 7 7
5 | 0 0 0 1 1 2 2 2 2 3 3 5 6 8 8 9
6 | 3 5
7 | 1 3
8 | 0 0 5 6
9 | 1
```

6 | 3 REPRESENTS
63 THUNDERSTORMS
PER YEAR

1. How does your city, or the city nearest you, compare to the other cities?

2. Which five cities have the largest number of days with thunderstorms? What do these five cities have in common?

3. The map on page 29 shows the United States divided into four regions: west, south, central, and northeast. Make a stem-and-leaf plot, replacing each city with the label for its location:
   W for WEST
   S for SOUTH
   C for CENTRAL
   N for NORTHEAST

4. Write a summary of what you can see in this stem-and-leaf plot.

Application 8

Married Teenagers

The table below gives the percentage of women aged 15–19 who are currently married in countries in the Western Hemisphere.

Country	Percentage of Women Aged 15–19 Currently Married
Argentina	10.1%
Bahamas	4.5
Barbados	0.6
Belize	8.9
Bolivia	15.6
Brazil	14.6
Canada	4.6
Chile	10.4
Columbia	—
Costa Rica	15.4
Cuba	26.9
Dominica	0.4
Dominican Republic	—
Ecuador	17.8
El Salvador	—
French Guiana	2.1
Grenada	0.5
Guadeloupe	1.4
Guatemala	26.4
Guyana	11.6
Haiti	8.0
Honduras	—
Jamaica	0.5
Martinique	0.5
Mexico	20.1
Nicaragua	—
Panama	20.1
Paraguay	14.1
Peru	14.2
Puerto Rico	13.6
St. Kitts and Nevis	0.5
St. Lucia	0.7
St. Vincent/Grenadines	1.3
Suriname	—
Trinidad and Tobago	11.3
United States	5.2
Uruguay	12.2
U.S. Virgin Islands	5.9
Venezuela	18.4

Source: United Nations, *The World's Women 1970-1990.*

31

(The information was not available for six countries so you will not be able to include them when you make the stem-and-leaf plot.)

1. These data are different from previous sets of data since the numbers contain decimals. The values go from 0.4 to 26.9, so we choose the stems to be 0, 1, 2, ..., 26. Copy and complete this stem-and-leaf plot of the percentages. The plot has been started with the values for Argentina and the Bahamas.

```
 0 |
 1 |
 2 |
 3 |
 4 | 5
 5 |
 6 |
 7 |
 8 |
 9 |
10 | 1
11 |
12 |
13 |
14 |
15 |
16 |
17 |
18 |
19 |
20 |
21 |
22 |
23 |
24 |
25 |
26 |
```

4 | 5 REPRESENTS
4.5 %

2. Label the United States.

3. Label the countries with the highest and lowest percentages.

4. Replace the leaves in your plot with the following symbols:
   I Caribbean countries
   S South American countries
   C Central American countries (including Mexico)
   N United States and Canada

5. Write a description of what you have learned from looking at the plots.

Back-to-Back Stem-and-Leaf Plots and Spreading Out Stem-and-Leaf Plots

Sometimes we want to compare two sets of data. For example, look at the following tables that contain the home run leaders for the National League and American League from 1921 to 1993.

	Home Run Leaders			
Year	National League	HR	American League	HR
1921	George Kelly, New York	23	Babe Ruth, New York	59
1922	Rogers Hornsby, St. Louis	42	Ken Williams, St. Louis	39
1923	Cy Williams, Philadelphia	41	Babe Ruth, New York	41
1924	Jacques Foumier, Brooklyn	27	Babe Ruth, New York	46
1925	Rogers Hornsby, St. Louis	39	Bob Meusel, New York	33
1926	Hack Wilson, Chicago	21	Babe Ruth, New York	47
1927	Hack Wilson, Chicago Cy Williams, Philadelphia	30	Babe Ruth, New York	60
1928	Hack Wilson, Chicago Jim Bottomley, St. Louis	31	Babe Ruth, New York	54
1929	Charles Klein, Philadelphia	43	Babe Ruth, New York	46
1930	Hack Wilson, Chicago	56	Babe Ruth, New York	49
1931	Charles Klein, Philadelphia	31	Babe Ruth, New York Lou Gehrig, New York	46
1932	Charles Klein, Philadelphia Mel Ott, New York	38	Jimmy Foxx, Philadelphia	58
1933	Charles Klein, Philadelphia	28	Jimmy Foxx, Philadelphia	48
1934	Rip Collins, St. Louis Mel Ott, New York	35	Lou Gehrig, New York	49
1935	Walter Berger, Boston	34	Jimmy Foxx, Philadelphia Hank Greenberg, Detroit	36
1936	Mel Ott, New York	33	Lou Gehrig, New York	49
1937	Mel Ott, New York Joe Medwick, St. Louis	31	Joe DiMaggio, New York	46
1938	Mel Ott, New York	36	Hank Greenberg, Detroit	58
1939	John Mize, St. Louis	28	Jimmy Foxx, Boston	35
1940	John Mize, St. Louis	43	Hank Greenberg, Detroit	41
1941	Dolph Camilli, Brooklyn	34	Ted Williams, Boston	37
1942	Mel Ott, New York	30	Ted Williams, Boston	36
1943	Bill Nicholson, Chicago	29	Rudy York, Detroit	34
1944	Bill Nicholson, Chicago	33	Nick Etten, New York	22
1945	Tommy Holmes, Boston	28	Vern Stephens, St. Louis	24
1946	Ralph Kiner, Pittsburgh	23	Hank Greenberg, Detroit	44
1947	Ralph Kiner, Pittsburgh John Mize, New York	51	Ted Williams, Boston	32
1948	Ralph Kiner, Pittsburgh John Mize, New York	40	Joe DiMaggio, New York	39
1949	Ralph Kiner, Pittsburgh	54	Ted Williams, Boston	43
1950	Ralph Kiner, Pittsburgh	47	Al Rosen, Cleveland	37
1951	Ralph Kiner, Pittsburgh	42	Gus Zernial, Chicago-Philadelphia	33
1952	Ralph Kiner, Pittsburgh Hank Sauer, Chicago	37	Larry Doby, Cleveland	32

Home Run Leaders — Continued

Year	National League	HR	American League	HR
1953	Ed Mathews, Milwaukee	47	Al Rosen, Cleveland	43
1954	Ted Kluszewski, Cincinnati	49	Larry Doby, Cleveland	32
1955	Willie Mays, New York	51	Mickey Mantle, New York	37
1956	Duke Snider, Brooklyn	43	Mickey Mantle, New York	52
1957	Hank Aaron, Milwaukee	44	Roy Sievers, Washington	42
1958	Ernie Banks, Chicago	47	Mickey Mantle, New York	42
1959	Ed Mathews, Milwaukee	46	Rocky Colavito, Cleveland Harmon Killebrew, Washington	42
1960	Ernie Banks, Chicago	41	Mickey Mantle, New York	40
1961	Orlando Cepeda, San Francisco	46	Roger Maris, New York	61
1962	Willie Mays, San Francisco	49	Harmon Killebrew, Minnesota	48
1963	Hank Aaron, Milwaukee Willie McCovey, San Francisco	44	Harmon Killebrew, Minnesota	45
1964	Willie Mays, San Francisco	47	Harmon Killebrew, Minnesota	49
1965	Willie Mays, San Francisco	52	Tony Conigliaro, Boston	32
1966	Hank Aaron, Atlanta	44	Frank Robinson, Baltimore	49
1967	Hank Aaron, Atlanta	39	Carl Yastrzemski, Boston Harmon Killebrew, Minnesota	44
1968	Willie McCovey, San Francisco	36	Frank Howard, Washington	44
1969	Willie McCovey, San Francisco	45	Harmon Killebrew, Minnesota	49
1970	Johnny Bench, Cincinnati	45	Frank Howard, Washington	44
1971	Willie Stargell, Pittsburgh	48	Bill Melton, Chicago	33
1972	Johnny Bench, Cincinnati	40	Dick Allen, Chicago	37
1973	Willie Stargell, Pittsburgh	44	Reggie Jackson, Oakland	32
1974	Mike Schmidt, Philadelphia	36	Dick Allen, Chicago	32
1975	Mike Schmidt, Philadelphia	38	George Scott, Milwaukee Reggie Jackson, Oakland	36
1976	Mike Schmidt, Philadelphia	38	Graig Nettles, New York	32
1977	George Foster, Cincinnati	52	Jim Rice, Boston	39
1978	George Foster, Cincinnati	40	Jim Rice, Boston	46
1979	Dave Kingman, Chicago	48	Gorman Thomas, Milwaukee	45
1980	Mike Schmidt, Philadelphia	48	Reggie Jackson, New York Ben Oglivie, Milwaukee	41
1981	Mike Schmidt, Philadelphia	31	Bobby Grich, California Tony Armas, Oakland Dwight Evans, Boston Eddie Murray, Baltimore	22
1982	Dave Kingman, New York	37	Gorman Thomas, Milwaukee Reggie Jackson, California	39
1983	Mike Schmidt, Philadelphia	40	Jim Rice, Boston	39
1984	Mike Schmidt, Philadelphia Dale Murphy, Atlanta	36	Tony Armas, Boston	43
1985	Dale Murphy, Atlanta	37	Darrell Evans, Detroit	40
1986	Mike Schmidt, Philadelphia	37	Jesse Barfield, Toronto	40
1987	Andre Dawson, Chicago	49	Mark McGwire, Oakland	49
1988	Darryl Strawberry, New York	39	Jose Canseco, Oakland	42
1989	Kevin Mitchell, San Francisco	47	Fred McGriff, Toronto	36
1990	Ryne Sandberg, Chicago	40	Cecil Fielder, Detroit	51
1991	Howard Johnson, New York	38	Jose Canseco, Oakland Cecil Fielder, Detroit	44
1992	Fred McGriff, San Diego	35	Juan Gonzales, Texas	43
1993	Barry Bonds, San Francisco	46	Juan Gonzales, Texas	46

In which league does the leader tend to hit more home runs? To find out, we make the following back-to-back stem-and-leaf plot of these data. Notice that the stems are in the center of the plot.

National League		American League
98887331	2	224
9998888777766665544331111 00	3	2222222333 4566667777 99999
99988877777666554444333 221100000	4	0001112222333344444 5566666678899999999
642211	5	124889
	6	01

| 2 | 4 REPRESENTS 24 HOME RUNS

There are too many leaves per stem, so we will spread out the stem-and-leaf plot using the stems below.

National League		American League
	2	
	·	
	3	
	·	
	4	
	·	
	5	
	·	
	6	

We will put the leaves 0, 1, 2, 3, and 4 on the first line for each stem and the leaves 5, 6, 7, 8, and 9 on the second line. The reorganized plot looks like this:

National League		American League
331	2	224
98887	·	
4433111100	3	2222223334
99988887777666655	·	566677779999
44443322110 0000	4	000111222233334 4444
99988877776665 5	·	5566666788999999 9
42211	5	124
6	·	889
	6	01

| 2 | 4 REPRESENTS 24 HOME RUNS

Discussion Questions

1. Does the American League champion or the National League champion tend to hit the most home runs?

2. Which three years were unusually low in home runs hit by the American League champion? What happened in these three years?

3. What shape is the distribution for each league?

4. Make a new back-to-back stem-and-leaf plot using the stems below. The home runs for the National League have been done for you. To construct this plot, you don't have to go back to the original list of data. Instead, take the values from one of the stem-and-leaf plots already constructed.

   For each stem, put the leaves:

   - 0 and 1 on the first line
   - 2 and 3 on the second line
   - 4 and 5 on the third line
   - 6 and 7 on the fourth line
   - 8 and 9 on the last line

National League		American League
1	2	
3 3	·	
	·	
7	·	
9 8 8	·	
1 1 1 1 0 0	3	
3 3	·	
5 5 4 4	·	
7 7 7 7 6 6 6 6	·	
9 9 9 8 8 8 8	·	
1 1 0 0 0 0 0	4	
3 3 3 2 2	·	
5 5 4 4 4 4	·	
7 7 7 7 6 6	·	
9 9 9 8 8 8	·	
1 1	5	
2 2	·	
4	·	
6	·	
	·	
	6	

9 | 3 | REPRESENTS 39 HOME RUNS

5. Which of the three back-to-back stem-and-leaf plots for the home run data do you think best displays the data? Why?

From a back-to-back plot like this, we can see that there tends to be a slightly larger number of home runs in the American League. We reach this conclusion because the values at the high end, in the upper 50's and 60's, come more often from the American League. Also, the values at the low end, in the 20's, come more often from the National League. For the stems in the 30's and the 40's, the number of leaves for the two leagues are about equal. The lower 50's has more values in the National League, but the American League makes up for this by having more values in the upper 50's and 60's.

Back-to-back stem-and-leaf plots are useful for comparing two sets of data. Before making comparisons, however,

- check to see first that both sets have about the same total number of values

- make sure that the plot is drawn accurately with each leaf taking up the same amount of space.

These checks are important because we make the comparisons mainly through comparing the numbers of leaves on both sides. If one side has more data values or each leaf takes more space on one side than on the other, it can be hard to make accurate comparisons. To get the sizes correct, it helps to construct the plot on graph paper.

To decide if one data set generally has larger values than the other, compare the number of leaves on the two sides for both the largest and smallest stems. Also, note if there are outliers or gaps in the data that are not the same on both sides, and whether or not the two sides have about the same shape.

Application 9

Traffic Deaths

The table below lists the 50 states and the District of Columbia with the number of deaths in a recent year per 100 million vehicle miles driven.

Motor Vehicle Traffic Deaths by State per 100 Million Vehicle Miles			
Alabama	2.6	Montana	2.5
Alaska	2.1	Nebraska	1.9
Arizona	2.5	Nevada	3.6
Arkansas	2.9	New Hampshire	1.6
California	2.0	New Jersey	1.5
Colorado	1.9	New Mexico	3.1
Connecticut	1.5	New York	2.0
Delaware	2.2	North Carolina	2.3
District of Columbia	1.6	North Dakota	1.9
Florida	2.7	Ohio	1.8
Georgia	2.0	Oklahoma	2.0
Hawaii	2.3	Oregon	2.2
Idaho	2.9	Pennsylvania	1.9
Illinois	1.9	Rhode Island	1.3
Indiana	1.8	South Carolina	2.9
Iowa	2.1	South Dakota	2.3
Kansas	2.1	Tennessee	2.6
Kentucky	2.6	Texas	2.0
Louisiana	2.5	Utah	2.0
Maine	1.8	Vermont	1.5
Maryland	1.9	Virginia	1.8
Massachusetts	1.3	Washington	1.9
Michigan	1.9	West Virginia	3.2
Minnesota	1.5	Wisconsin	1.8
Mississippi	3.2	Wyoming	2.2
Missouri	2.3		

Source: National Safety Council.

1. If a state had 685 traffic deaths for 20,000,000,000 vehicle miles, what rate would be listed in the table above?

2. If Alabama had a total of 735 auto deaths during the year, how many miles were driven in Alabama that year?

3. How do the states in the south compare with those in the northeast? To decide, construct a back-to-back stem-and-leaf plot with the stems spread out. Use the map on page 29 to determine which 13 states are in the South and which 12 states and district are in the northeast.

38

4. Which state in the northeast might be considered an outlier?

5. Which two of the other states in the northeast have high traffic death rates? Would you call them outliers?

6. Do states in the south or in the northeast generally have higher traffic death rates?

7. Summarize what you learned from this back-to-back stem-and-leaf plot.

8. What factors do you think might help to explain the difference between the south and the northeast?

9. (For class discussion) How could these data have been collected?

Stem-and-Leaf Plots Where the Data Should be Truncated

The following table lists the percentage of newborn babies in each state who weigh less than 5 pounds 8 ounces.

Births with Low Birth Weight as a Percent of Live Births

State	Percent	State	Percent
South Carolina	8.95%	Connecticut	6.74%
Louisiana	8.80	Kentucky	6.70
Mississippi	8.72	Indiana	6.57
Georgia	8.36	Oklahoma	6.54
Arkansas	8.19	West Virginia	6.36
Maryland	8.10	Arizona	6.23
North Carolina	8.02	Kansas	6.13
Alabama	8.01	Rhode Island	6.00
Tennessee	7.86	California	6.00
Colorado	7.84	Massachusetts	5.99
New York	7.76	Montana	5.95
Florida	7.67	Utah	5.68
Nevada	7.54	Nebraska	5.52
Illinois	7.46	Wisconsin	5.45
Delaware	7.35	Iowa	5.44
Michigan	7.29	Washington	5.25
New Mexico	7.22	Oregon	5.25
Wyoming	7.04	Idaho	5.13
New Jersey	7.04	Vermont	5.01
Virginia	7.03	Minnesota	4.98
Pennsylvania	6.89	Alaska	4.97
Hawaii	6.88	Maine	4.85
Ohio	6.86	New Hampshire	4.82
Texas	6.83	North Dakota	4.80
Missouri	6.83	South Dakota	4.67

Source: National Center for Health Statistics, *Vital Statistics of the United States.*

The highest percentage, for South Carolina, is 8.95. The lowest, for South Dakota, is 4.67. Start the stem-and-leaf plot as follows:

```
4 |
  .
5 |
  .
6 |
  .
7 |
  .
8 |
  .
```

To place South Carolina's 8.95 on the plot, truncate (cut off) the last digit. This leaves 8.9, which goes on the plot as follows:

```
4 |
  · |
5 |
  · |
6 |
  · |
7 |
  · |
8 |
  · | 9
```

The finished plot follows.

```
4 |
  · | 6 8 8 8 9 9
5 | 0 1 2 2 4 4
  · | 5 6 9 9
6 | 0 0 1 2 3
  · | 5 5 7 7 8 8 8 8 8
7 | 0 0 0 2 2 3 4
  · | 5 6 7 8 8
8 | 0 0 1 1 3
  · | 7 8 9
```

4 | 8 REPRESENTS
4.80 - 4.89%

Discussion Questions

1. What percentages can 8|5 represent? 6|1?

2. Make a back-to-back stem-and-leaf plot to compare the 13 southern states with the other 37 states. Use the map on page 29.

   Since there are 13 southern states and 37 non-southern states, we need to make a mental adjustment for this fact and concentrate on the location, spread, and shape of the two distributions.

3. Which non-southern state has the highest percentage? Which southern state has the lowest percentage? What observation can you make about these two states?

4. Write several sentences about what you see in the plot you constructed in question 2.

5. In the previous stem-and-leaf plots, the percentages were truncated. Instead of truncating, we will now *round* each percentage to the nearest tenth. Then we will see if the back-to-back stem-and-leaf plot gives the same impression as before. The Other States side of the plot below was made by rounding. Copy the plot and complete the Southern States side using rounding. The symbol 4|8 now represents 4.75% to 4.84%.

Southern States		Other States
	4	
	·	6 8 8 8 9 9
	5	0 1 2 2 4 4
	·	5 6 9 9
	6	0 0 1 2 3
	·	5 7 8 8 8 8
	7	0 0 2 2 3 4
	·	5 7 8
	8	1
	·	

6. Is it faster to round or to truncate?

7. Does the back-to-back stem-and-leaf plot with rounded numbers give the same general impression as the one with truncated numbers? Are there any differences in what you learn from the two plots?

8. Do you think truncating is an appropriate procedure, or should the data be rounded?

If you are like many students, you may feel that there is something wrong about truncating. It seems less accurate than rounding, and therefore worse. But is using 4|8 to represent 4.75% to 4.84% really more accurate for our purposes than using 4|8 to represent 4.80% to 4.89%? Another point to consider is that the data we have may already be either rounded or truncated, and we don't know which.

Finally, it is easy to make a mistake when rounding. In order to truncate, all we do is use a straightedge to cover the columns of digits not needed. To decide if truncating is appropriate for a specific problem, ask yourself if it is likely to make any difference in the interpretations you reach.

Possible project: Investigate the causes of low birth weight in babies. What women are most likely to have low-birth-weight babies? In what ways are low-birth-weight babies at risk? Why do southern states have higher percentages of low-birth-weight babies? The percentage for the District of Columbia is 14.30%. Is this rate typical of urban areas?

Application 10

Children's Books

The following table lists the children's books published in the United States since 1895 that have sold one million or more copies.

Best-Selling Children's Books
Published In United States as of 1977

Book	Copies Sold
Green Eggs and Ham, by Dr. Seuss. 1960	5,940,776
One Fish, Two Fish, Red Fish, Blue Fish, by Dr. Seuss. 1960	5,842,024
Hop on Pop, by Dr. Seuss. 1963	5,814,101
Dr. Seuss' ABC, by Dr. Seuss. 1963	5,648,193
The Cat in the Hat, by Dr. Seuss. 1957	5,394,741
The Wonderful Wizard of Oz, by L. Frank Baum. 1900 (estimate)	5,000,000
Charlotte's Web, by E. B. White. 1952	4,670,516
The Cat in the Hat Comes Back, by Dr. Seuss. 1958	3,431,917
The Little Prince, by Antoine de Saint-Exupery. 1943	2,811,478
The Little House on the Prairie, by Laura Ingalls Wilder. 1953 edition	2,732,666
The Little House in the Big Woods, by Laura Ingalls Wilder. 1953 edition	2,527,203
My First Atlas. 1959	2,431,000
Love and the Facts of Life, by Evelyn Duvall and Sylvanus Duvall. 1950	2,360,000
Egermeier's Bible Story Book, by Elsie E. Egermeier. 1923	2,326,577
Go Ask Alice, Anonymous. 1971	2,245,605
Benji, by Leonore Fleischer. 1974	2,235,694
The Little Engine That Could, by Watty Piper. 1926	2,166,000
Stuart Little, by E. B. White. 1945	2,129,591
Freckles, by Gene Stratton Potter. 1904	2,089,523
The Girl of the Limberlost, by Gene Stratton Porter. 1909	2,053,892
Sounder, by William Armstrong. 1969	1,815,401
Harry, the Dirty Dog, by Gene Zion. 1956	1,690,339
Seventeen, by Booth Tarkington. 1916 (estimate)	1,682,891
Where the Wild Things Are, by Maurice Sendak. 1963	1,632,020
Laddie, by Gene Stratton Porter. 1913	1,586,529
The Big Book of Mother Goose, 1950	1,500,000
The Golden Dictionary, by Ellen Wales Walpole. 1944	1,450,000
A Friend is Someone Who Likes You, by Joan Walsh Anglund. 1958	1,423,432
Rebecca of Sunnybrook Farm, by Kate Douglas Wiggin. 1904	1,357,714
Love Is a Special Way of Feeling, by Joan Walsh Anglund. 1960	1,308,293

Best-Selling Children's Books
Published in United States — Continued

Book	Copies Sold
The Real Mother Goose. 1915	1,296,140
The Pigman, by Paul Zindel. 1968	1,265,876
Better Homes and Gardens Story Book. 1951	1,220,728
Trouble After School, by Jerrold Beim. 1957	1,145,570
Better Homes and Gardens Junior Cook Book. 1955	1,100,182
Pollyanna, by Eleanor H. Porter. 1913	1,059,000
Le Petit Prince, by Antoine de Saint-Exupery. 1943	1,018,373
Mary Poppins, by Pamela L. Travers. 1934	1,005,203
Winnie-the-Pooh, by A. A. Milne. 1926	1,005,000
Pollyanna Grows Up, by Eleanor H. Porter. 1915	1,000,000

Source: A. P. Hackett and J. H. Burke, *Eighty Years of Best Sellers.*

1. Make a stem-and-leaf plot of these data. Truncate all digits except those in the millions and hundred-thousands places.

2. Underline all digits representing books by Dr. Seuss.

3. Circle the digits representing the books you have read. Do these circles tend to be at the top or the bottom of the diagram? Why?

4. If another line were added to the top of the plot for books which sold 500,000–999,999 copies, how long do you think it would be? Why?

5. Write a summary of the information displayed in the plot.

Stem-and-Leaf Plots — Summary

Stem-and-leaf plots are a new way to quickly organize and display data. They were invented by John Tukey around 1970. Statisticians use stem-and-leaf plots as a substitute for the less informative histograms and bar graphs. All individual values are displayed on a stem-and-leaf plot so it is easy to spot the relative location of any particular individual value we are interested in.

You should know how to construct the following variations of stem-and-leaf plots.

- back-to-back
- truncated and rounded
- spread-out

From a stem-and-leaf plot, it is easy to identify the largest and smallest values, outliers, clusters, gaps, the relative position of any important value, and the shape of the distribution.

Suggestions for Student Projects

1. Collect data on a topic that interests you, make a stem-and-leaf plot, and then write a summary of the information displayed in the plot. Use one of the topics listed below or think of your own.

   a. Compare the ages in months of the boys and the girls in your class.

   b. Compare the heights of the boys and the girls in your class.

   c. Compare the gas mileage of foreign and domestic cars. (This information can be found in many almanacs.)

   d. Compare the scores of two different classes taking the same math test.

   The next two projects involve comparing number line plots with stem-and-leaf plots.

2. Devise a way to use symbols in a number line plot to replace the individual data values, as we did for the stem-and-leaf plots in the fast foods and thunderstorm examples. Then, construct a number line plot for one of these examples, using your method. Do the number line and stem-and-leaf plots show any different information? Which is easier to interpret? Which do you prefer?

3. Devise a way of modifying a number line plot to get a back-to-back plot. Then redo Application 9 using your back-to-back plot. Which is easier to construct, the back-to-back number line plot or the back-to-back stem-and-leaf plot? Do they show different information? Which shows the information more clearly? Which do you prefer? Can you think of situations in which you might prefer the other plot?

4. To compare truncating and rounding, take any of the data in this section and make a back-to-back stem-and-leaf plot of the truncated against the rounded values. Do you see any difference, and if so what is it? Could you have predicted this?

5. In the Burger King example at the beginning of this section, we showed the type of food in the stem-and-leaf plot by replacing the leaves with letters. A way to show both the specific numerical values and labels is to keep the numerical leaf in the plot and follow it by a label in parentheses. For instance, the third-from-bottom row in the plot of fat would be

$$3 \mid 1(H),\ 2(S),\ 3(H),\ 8(H)$$

By keeping the number in the plot, we retain as much detailed numerical information as is generally needed. This idea is especially useful for displaying data where there is one number for each of the 50 states. The two-letter postal abbreviation can be used to identify each state. Find some interesting data where there is one value for each state. A good example would be each state's current population as found in an almanac. Make the plot just described, and write a summary of the information displayed.

IV. MEDIAN, MEAN, QUARTILES, AND OUTLIERS

Median and Mean

You have probably learned how to compute the average of a set of numbers. For example, if Mary gets scores of 80, 96, 84, 95, and 90 on five math tests, then her average is:

$$\frac{80 + 96 + 84 + 95 + 90}{5}$$

$$= \frac{445}{5}$$

$$= 89.$$

Whenever we compute an average this way, we will call it the *mean*. Thus, the mean of Mary's test scores is 89. We need a new word for the average because there are other kinds of averages. Another type of average is the *median*. To find the median of Mary's test scores, first put them in order from smallest to largest.

$$80 \quad 84 \quad \boxed{90} \quad 95 \quad 96$$

The middle score, 90, is the median. Half of Mary's five test scores are lower than or equal to the median and half are higher than or equal to the median.

What do we do if there is an even number of scores? If Mary takes a sixth test and gets a 25, her scores are now:

$$25 \quad 80 \quad \boxed{84 \quad 90} \quad 95 \quad 96.$$

There are two scores in the middle, 84 and 90. The median is halfway between these two scores:

$$\frac{84 + 90}{2}$$

$$= \frac{174}{2}$$

$$= 87.$$

Half of her six test scores are lower than 87 and half are higher.

Discussion Questions

1. Compute the mean of Mary's six test scores.

2. On the basis of this grading scale, what grade would Mary receive if the mean of the six tests is used to determine her grade?

   A 90–100   B 80–89   C 70–79   D 60–69   F 0–59

3. What grade would she receive if the median of the six tests is used to determine her grade?

4. Does one extreme score cause a greater change in the median or in the mean?

5. Do you need to know all of the data values in order to find the median? For example, suppose that Mary has taken 6 tests and you only know 5 of her scores. Can you calculate the median?

6. Give a reason for choosing the median to summarize Mary's test scores.

7. Give a reason for choosing the mean to summarize Mary's test scores.

8. Which do you think is better to use, the mean or median?

9. Why do you think the median rather than the mean was used in the following examples?

   a. According to the U.S. Bureau of the Census, the median age at first marriage for men is 26.3 years and for women is 24.1 years.

   b. According to the U.S. Bureau of Labor, the median family income in the United States is $34,788 per year.

   c. According to the Bureau of the Census, the median amount of time spent weekly on homework for students in American private high schools is 14.2 hours—their public-school counterparts, in comparison, spend 6.5 hours weekly on homework.

   d. The median-priced single-family home in the United States costs $79,100.

   e. The National Education Association reports that the median age for a public school teacher is 41 years.

   f. In 1993, *Zillions* magazine surveyed 692 kids across the country about their weekly allowances. They found that half of the kids surveyed received allowances:

      Weekly
      Allowance*
      | $2 | 9- and 10-year-olds |
      | $5 | 11- and 12-year olds |
      | $5 | 13- and 14-year-olds |

      * The amounts shown here are median amounts.

9- and 10-
year-olds   11- and 12-
year-olds   13- and 14-
year-olds

10. In the following newspaper story, what do you think is the meaning of the word *average*? Give your reasons.

"[In a study of jury awards in civil trials, it was] found that while the average award against corporate defendants was more than $120,000, the average against individuals was $18,500. The average against government defendants was $38,000, but it was $97,000 in cases that involved hospitals and other nonprofit entities.

"'To some degree, the average awards against corporations and hospitals were so great because of a few extraordinarily large awards,' the report explained." (*Newark Star-Ledger*, August 20, 1985)

11. The following are examples of information that seem to be incorrect:

"According to the latest enrollment analysis by age-categories, half of the [Los Angeles Community College] district's 128,000 students are over the age of 24. The average student is 29." (*Los Angeles Times*, September 20, 1981.)

"In the region we are traveling west of Whitney, precipitation drops off and the average snow depth on April 1 for the southern Sierra is a modest 5 to 6 feet. And two winters out of three, the snow pack is below average." (Ezra Bowen, *The High Sierra* (New York: Time-Life Books, 1972), p. 142.)

The average sale price of a house in the San Fernando Valley in August was $247,900. The median price was $199,000. (*Los Angeles Times*, October 3, 1992.)

a. Give an example of four students with a mean age of 29 and median age of 24.

      b.   Give an example of the snow depth for three winters that makes the quote from *The High Sierra* true.

      c.   Give an example of five selling prices that would have a mean of $247,900 and a median of $199,000.

12. Construct a set of data where neither the mean nor the median is a reasonable "typical" value.

13. There is an old joke about a student who transferred from the University of California at Los Angeles to the University of Southern California and raised the average GPA (grade point average) at both schools. Is this possible? Explain.

14. Barbara's grades on her first four math tests are 90, 85, 92, and 87. What score must she get on the fifth test to make her average 90?

Both the median and the mean summarize the data by giving a measure of the center of the data values. Which you use depends on your purpose in finding a measure of center. When there are no outliers, there generally will not be much difference between the median and the mean, and which you choose won't matter much.

Using a calculator, the mean is easy to compute. To find the median, however, the data must be ordered from smallest to largest, which is done most quickly by constructing a stem-and-leaf plot.

Neither the median nor the mean can tell us as much about the data as a plot showing all the values, such as a number line plot, a dot plot, or a stem-and-leaf plot.

Application 11

How Many Moons?

A visitor from the star Alpha Centauri has selected you to provide her with information about our solar system. She is filling out a form and asks how many moons are "average" for a planet in our solar system.

Study the table below.

Planet	Number of Moons	Approximate Length of a Day in Earth Hours
Mercury	0	1,416
Venus	0	5,832
Earth	1	24
Mars	2	24.5
Jupiter	16	10
Saturn	23	11
Uranus	15	17
Neptune	8	16
Pluto	1	153

1. Compute the mean number of moons.

2. Compute the median number of moons.

3. Which three planets are the most different in number of moons compared to the others? Do you know any explanation for this?

4. Do you think the visitor from Alpha Centauri would get a more accurate impression about the typical number of moons from the median or the mean? Is either summary number adequate? Give your reasons.

Next, the visitor asks about the length of a typical day in our solar system.

5. Compute the mean length of a day in our solar system in hours.

6. How many Earth days is this?

7. Find the median length of a day in our solar system.

8. Do you think it is better to give your visitor the mean length of a day or the median length of a day? Why? Are you happy about giving your visitor one single number? Why or why not?

Application 12

Rating Television Shows

List five current television shows in the boxes on the left of the chart. Select six students to rate them. The six students and your teacher should give each show a rating from 0 to 100 according to the scale below. Do this independently; each rater should not know the ratings of the others until everyone is finished.

TV Shows	Student #1	Student #2	Student #3	Student #4	Student #5	Student #6	Your Teacher

The ratings system: 90–100, excellent; 70–89, good; 50–69, fair; 30–49, weak; 0–29, terrible.

1. Compute the mean rating for each show.

2. Compute the median rating for each show.

3. a) For which show are the mean and median farthest apart?

   b) Which reviewer caused this?

   c) Is the mean or the median more representative of this show's overall rating?

4. a) If you judge by the mean rating, which reviewer is the hardest grader?

   b) If you judge by the median rating, which reviewer is the hardest grader?

   c) Which reviewer tends to be the most different from the others?

Range, Quartiles, and Interquartile Range

The number of grams of fat in a 3-ounce (85 gram) serving of 13 kinds of meat is show below.

Meat	Grams of Fat	Meat	Grams of Fat
Ham	14	Beef liver	7
Bacon	40	Sirloin steak	15
Fried pork chop	26	Fatty beef roast	26
Lean beef roast	12	Dry salami	30
Lean ground beef	16	Veal cutlet	9
Regular ground beef	18	Bologna	24
		Frankfurter	25

Source: U.S. Department of Agriculture.

To find the *range,* subtract the smallest number from the largest. The range for the grams of fat is:

$$40 - 7 = 33 \text{ grams.}$$

We will also learn how to find the *lower quartile* and the *upper quartile.* If the numbers are arranged in order from smallest to largest, the lower quartile, the median, and the upper quartile divide them into four groups of roughly the same size.

X X X X X X X X X X X X X X X X X X X X X X X X X X

| Lower | Lower | Median | Upper | Upper |
| Extreme | Quartile | | Quartile | Extreme |

To find the quartiles of the previous numbers, first arrange the numbers in order:

7   9   12   14   15   16   18   24   25   26   26   30   40

Second, find the median and draw a vertical line through it.

7   9   12   14   15   16   1|8   24   25   26   26   30   40

The median is 18. Six numbers are below this 18 and six are above it.

Third, consider only the data values to the left of the line and find their median.

7   9   12|14   15   16

The median of these six numbers is between 12 and 14. This is the lower quartile. Thus, the lower quartile is 13. We have drawn a vertical line at the median of these values in the same way as before.

Finally, consider only the data values to the right of the line and find their median. This is the upper quartile. The upper quartile is 26.

$$24 \quad 25 \quad 26 \mid 26 \quad 30 \quad 40$$

We have divided the numbers into four groups:

$$7 \quad 9 \quad 12 \mid 14 \quad 15 \quad 16 \quad 1 \mid 8 \quad 24 \quad 25 \quad 26 \mid 26 \quad 30 \quad 40$$

Notice that there are three numbers in each group.

The *interquartile range* is the difference of the upper quartile and the lower quartile. The interquartile range of the given numbers is:

$$26 - 13 = 13.$$

The *lower extreme* is the smallest value in the data. In this case, it is 7. Similarly, the *upper extreme* is the largest number in the data. In this case, it is 40.

The fastest way to order the numbers from smallest to largest is to make a stem-and-leaf plot of the data, with the leaves ordered. Then, count in from the top and bottom to mark the median and quartiles. As an example, suppose we did not have frankfurter in the list of meats and we wanted the median and quartiles of the remaining 12 meats. The median will then be between the sixth and seventh values. We draw the first line there and consider only the data values below and above this line, as before, to get the quartiles.

```
0 | 7 9
1 | 2 ¦4 5 6¦8
2 | 4 6¦6
3 | 0
4 | 0
```

The vertical lines here are dotted. The median is 17, the lower quartile is 13, and the upper quartile is 26.

Discussion Questions

1. In these data, the median and quartiles are all whole numbers. Find a set of 13 whole numbers where the quartiles are not whole numbers.

2. Is the interquartile range half of the range?

3. Cross the 40 grams from bacon off the original list and find the new median and quartiles.

4. By how much did these values change?

5. Recompute the range and interquartile range.

6. By how much did these values change?

7. Find two different sets of seven numbers with:

lower extreme -   3
lower quartile -   5
median - 10
upper quartile - 12
upper extreme - 13

8. The median is always between the two quartiles. Find a set of seven numbers where the mean is above the upper quartile.

9. Find a set of seven numbers where the mean is below the lower quartile.

10. Each gram of fat produces 9 calories. Three ounces of sirloin steak has 240 calories. What percentage of the calories come from fat?

11. Three ounces of lean ground beef has 230 calories. What percentage of the calories come from fat?

12. The table below gives the recommended daily dietary allowance (RDA) of food energy (calories) for maintenance of good nutrition.

Males		Females	
Age	Calories	Age	Calories
11–14	2,700	11–14	2,200
15–18	2,800	15–18	2,100
19–22	2,900	19–22	2,100
23–50	2,700	23–50	2,000

Source: U.S. Department of Agriculture, *Nutritive Value of Foods.*

If you want your diet to have no more than 30% of its calories come from fat, how many grams of fat can you eat per day?

13. For additional practice, find the median, quartiles, and extremes of the following:

    a. the ages of U.S. presidents at their deaths (Application 6)

    b. the percentage of women aged 15–19 who are married (Application 8)

Application 13

Ice Cream Prices

The table below gives the prices for half of a gallon of all of the different kinds of ice cream and ice milk/dairy desserts sold at a Los Angeles supermarket.

Ice Cream	Price for Half a Gallon
Ben and Jerry's	$11.80
Breyer's	4.65
Dreyer's Grand	4.79
Frusen Gladje	10.76
Haagen Dazs	9.98
Jerseymaid	2.65
Jerseymaid Natural	2.50
Jerseymaid Old Fashioned	2.50
McConnell's	9.96
Mrs. Field's	4.69
Royal Request	9.38
Westwood	2.45

Ice Milk/Dairy Desserts	Price for Half a Gallon
Breyer's Natural Light	$4.85
Dreyer's Grand Light	4.79
Jerseymaid Lightly Maid	2.85
Jerseymaid Light	3.85
Lean Cuisine	4.75
Weight Watchers	10.36

1. Find the mean price of a half gallon of ice cream.

2. Find the mean price of a half gallon of ice milk/dairy dessert.

3. Find the median price of a half gallon of ice cream.

4. Find the median price of a half gallon of ice milk/dairy dessert.

5. Does the mean or the median give a better indication of the typical price of a half gallon of ice cream? of ice milk/dairy dessert? Explain.

6. In general, which type is more expensive? Try to find out why this is the case and how ice cream, ice milk, and dairy desserts differ.

For the rest of the questions, combine both lists.

7. What is the range in prices of all 18 brands?

8. Find the lower quartile of all 18 brands.

9. Find the upper quartile.

10. What is the interquartile range of the prices?

11. Write a paragraph for a student who is absent about how to find the interquartile range of the prices and what the interquartile range tells us.

Possible project: How many single-scoop cones can be made from a half gallon? How does the price of a single-scoop cone made at home compare to the price of a single scoop at an ice cream shop?

Outliers

The following table lists all 15 records that reached Number 1 for the first time in 1959, and the total number of weeks that each record held the Number 1 spot.

Weeks	Record Title	Artist
3	"Smoke Gets in Your Eyes"	Platters
4	"Stagger Lee"	Lloyd Price
5	"Venus"	Frankie Avalon
4	"Come Softly to Me"	Fleetwoods
1	"The Happy Organ"	Dave 'Baby' Cortez
2	"Kansas City"	Wilbert Harrison
6	"The Battle of New Orleans"	Johnny Horton
4	"Lonely Boy"	Paul Anka
2	"A Big Hunk o' Love"	Elvis Presley
4	"The Three Bells"	Browns
2	"Sleep Walk"	Santo & Johnny
9	"Mack the Knife"	Bobby Darin
1	"Mr. Blue"	Fleetwoods
2	"Heartaches by the Number"	Guy Mitchell
1	"Why"	Frankie Avalon

Source: *The Billboard Book of Top 40 Hits*, 1985.

We have already used the word *outlier* several times to indicate values that are widely separated from the rest of the data. Would you say that any record in the list above is an outlier? If we think we have spotted an outlier, it is worth some special thought about why it is different from the rest. Trying to make sense out of the outliers can be an important part of interpreting data.

It is not reasonable, however, to automatically call the upper and lower extremes outliers. Any data set has extremes, and we don't want to put extra energy into trying to interpret them unless they are separated from the rest of the data. We could decide if an observation is an outlier by looking at a plot and making a decision, as we have done so far. However, it is helpful to have a rule to aid in making the decision, especially when there are a moderate to large number of observations (say 25 or more).

Thus, we say that an *outlier* is any number more than 1.5 interquartile ranges above the upper quartile, or more than 1.5 interquartile ranges below the lower quartile. A number line plot of the hit record data, with the median (M) and quartiles (LQ and UQ) labeled, follows.

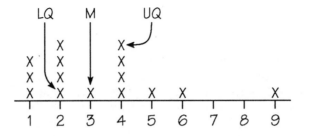

The interquartile range (IQR) is 4 − 2 = 2, so 1.5 × IQR = 3. Thus, the upper cut-off is 4 + 3 = 7. Since the data value 9 ("Mack the Knife") is greater than 7, we call it an outlier. For the lower end, the cut-off is 2 − 3 = −1. Since no data value can be less than −1, there are no outliers at the lower end. An interpretation we can draw is that "Mack the Knife" was not only the most popular record in 1959, but that it really stands out as substantially more popular than the other 14 top hits. Before doing this calculation, did you feel that "Mack the Knife" was an outlier?

The rule just described is quick, easy, and straightforward to use. Multiplying the IQR by 1.5 rather than 1.0 or 2.0 generally produces results that are what we would like, if we were to decide which values should be labeled outliers. You might experiment using multipliers such as 1.0, 1.5, and 2.0 to decide which you prefer. Different situations can call for different rules.

Application 14

Prices of Blue Jeans

The following table gives the regular price (to the nearest dollar) of the blue jeans that could be found in the junior women and young men departments of the stores in a large Los Angeles mall. Different stores often had different prices for the same style jeans. The cheapest price is given below. The jeans were all medium blue in color and made in the five-pocket, zipper-fly style commonly called "standard," "classic," or "basic." (Styles such as baggy or button-fly tended to be more expensive.)

Young Men's Brands		Junior Women's Brands	
Arizona	$22.00	Bongo	$30.00
Blue Stone	40.00	Contempo's Nada Nuff	20.00
B.U.M.	40.00	Cross Colours	54.00
Cosi	33.00	Dakota Blue	34.00
Eddie Bauer	30.00	Eddie Bauer	30.00
Gap Easy Fit	34.00	Esprit Classic	50.00
Guess Basic	56.00	Gap Classic Fit	34.00
Guess Five-pocket	56.00	Gap Easy Fit	34.00
Index Internationale	30.00	Guess Basic	56.00
Lee Easy Riders	32.00	Jordache Basics	25.00
Lee Storm Riders	25.00	Lee Basics	30.00
Levi's 505	32.00	Lee Easy Rider	30.00
Levi's 512	35.00	I.e.i.	29.00
Levi's 550	40.00	Levi's 512	38.00
Levi's SilverTab	44.00	Levi's 550	42.00
Marithe Francois Girbaud	62.00	Miller's Outpost Anchor Blue	28.00
Miller's Outpost Anchor Blue	34.00	Mixed Blues	20.00
Umen	33.00	No!	30.00
		No Excuses	22.00
		Paris Blues	29.00
		Rio	25.00
		The Limited's Five Pocket	36.00
		Union Bay	44.00
		Whooz Blooz	39.00
		Z. Cavaricci	60.00
		Zena	48.00

1. Make a back-to-back stem-and-leaf plot of the prices for young men and for young women.

2. Are there any gaps in the prices? If so, where?

3. For the prices of jeans for young women,

   a. Compute the mean price.

    b. Find the median price.

    c. Why is the mean price larger than the median price?

    d. Find the quartiles.

    e. Find the interquartile range.

    f. Use the $1.5 \times$ IQR rule to find any outliers.

4. For the prices of jeans for young men,

    a. Predict whether the mean price or median price will be greater.

    b. Find the mean price and median price to check your prediction.

    c. Find the quartiles.

    d. Find the interquartile range.

    e. Use the $1.5 \times$ IQR rule to find any outliers.

    f. If you remove the three outliers from the list of prices, do you think the mean or the median will decrease the most?

    g. Cross off the three outliers from the list. Find the mean and median of the remaining 15 prices. Which decreased more, the mean or the median?

5. Find the range in prices for young women's jeans.

Median, Mean, Quartiles, and Outliers — Summary

Both the median and the mean are single numbers that summarize the location of the data. Neither alone can tell the whole story about the data, but sometimes we do want a single, concise, summary value. Generally, the median is more valuable than the mean, especially if there is any possibility of having even a few unusually large or small values in the data. Also, we know that about half the values lie below the median and about half lie above the median. We can make no comparable statement about the mean.

The lower quartile, median, and upper quartile divide the data into four parts with approximately the same number of observations in each part. The interquartile range (IQR), the third quartile minus the first quartile, is a measure of how spread out the data are. If a number is more than 1.5 times the interquartile range above the upper quartile or below the lower quartile, we call it an outlier. If the data are grouped fairly tightly, there will be no outliers. When we do find an outlier, we should study it closely. It is worthwhile to try to find reasons for it, as it can be an important part of the overall interpretation of the data.

Suggestions for Student Projects

1. When talking to friends, the average person says "um" about twice a minute. There is some evidence that math and science teachers average fewer "ums" per minute than social science and humanities teachers (*Los Angeles Times*, April 27, 1992). The hypothesis is that people who are weighing their verbal options while speaking tend to say "um" more often. Design a study to compare the number of "um"s said per minute by two different groups of people. Look at the means, medians, quartiles, and extremes.

2. Find examples of the use of the words *mean, median,* or *average* in a local newspaper. If you find *average,* can you tell if it refers to the median, the mean, or some other method? If you find *mean* or *median,* discuss whether or not the appropriate method was used.

3. The following data from *The Billboard Book of Top 40 Hits* give the Number 1 hit records in 1966. Make a number line plot and identify any outliers using several different rules (for example, multipliers of 1.0, 1.5, and 2.0, or other appropriate multipliers). Then, decide which rule you like the best for these data.

4. Try the different multipliers on other sets of data. What is your choice for the most appropriate multiplier?

1966 Number 1 Hit Records

Weeks	Record Title	Artist
2	"The Sounds of Silence"	Simon & Garfunkel
3	"We Can Work It Out"	Beatles
2	"My Love"	Petula Clark
1	"Lightnin' Strikes"	Lou Christie
1	"These Boots Are Made for Walkin'"	Nancy Sinatra
5	"The Ballad of the Green Berets"	Sgt. Barry Sadler
3	"(You're My) Soul and Inspiration"	Righteous Brothers
1	"Good Lovin'"	Young Rascals
3	"Monday, Monday"	The Mamas & The Papas
2	"When a Man Loves a Woman"	Percy Sledge
2	"Paint It Black"	Rolling Stones
2	"Paperback Writer"	Beatles
1	"Strangers in the Night"	Frank Sinatra
2	"Hanky Panky"	Tommy James & The Shondells
2	"Wild Thing"	Troggs
3	"Summer in the City"	Lovin' Spoonful
1	"Sunshine Superman"	Donovan
2	"You Can't Hurry Love"	Supremes
3	"Cherish"	Association
2	"Reach Out I'll Be There"	Four Tops
1	"96 Tears"	? & The Mysterians
1	"Last Train to Clarksville"	Monkees
1	"Poor Side of Town"	Johnny Rivers
2	"You Keep Me Hangin' On"	Supremes
3	"Winchester Cathedral"	New Vaudeville Band
1	"Good Vibrations"	Beach Boys
7	"I'm a Believer"	Monkees

Source: *The Billboard Book of Top 40 Hits*, 1985.

V. BOX PLOTS

In the last section, we learned how to find the extremes, the quartiles, and the median. These five numbers tell us a great deal about a set of data. In this section, we will describe a way of using them to make a box plot for a data set with a large number of values.

The following table gives the results of federal crash tests for 1993 cars sold in the United States. The cars were crashed into a wall at 35 miles per hour with a dummy wearing the seat belt and shoulder harness. A "Driver Head Injury" score of 500 or less means that there was almost no chance of a driver getting a serious head injury. A higher score means more chance of a serious head injury. A score of 1,000 means there is about one chance in six. The following table also tells whether the car comes equipped with a driver's side air bag.

Make and Model	Driver Head Injury	Driver Air Bag?
Acura Integra	585	No
Acura Legend	897	Yes
BMW 325i	705	Yes
Buick Century Custom	542	Yes
Buick Regal	880	No
Chevrolet Astro Van	2,065	No
Chevrolet Beretta	343	Yes
Chevrolet Caprice	533	Yes
Chevrolet Cavalier	770	No
Chevrolet Corsica	493	Yes
Chevrolet Geo Metro	860	No
Chevrolet Geo Storm	417	Yes
Chrysler Concorde	770	Yes
Chrysler New Yorker	674	Yes
Dodge Caravan van	407	Yes
Dodge/Plymouth Colt	919	No
Dodge Daytona	399	Yes
Dodge Dynasty	674	Yes
Dodge Intrepid	770	Yes
Dodge Shadow	503	Yes
Eagle Vision	770	Yes
Ford Aerostar van	485	Yes
Ford Crown Victoria	907	Yes
Ford Mustang	651	Yes
Ford Probe	784	Yes
Ford Taurus	647	Yes
Ford Taurus wagon	480	Yes
Ford Thunderbird	541	No
Honda Accord	501	Yes
Honda Accord SE	555	Yes
Honda Civic	744	Yes
Honda Prelude	510	Yes
Hyundai Excel sedan	696	No
Hyundai Excel hatch	520	No
Hyundai Scoupe	870	No

Lincoln Continental	863	Yes
Mazda 626	589	Yes
Mazda Miata	920	Yes
Mazda Protege	779	No
Mitsubishi Eclipse	772	No
Mitsubishi Galant	1,024	No
Mitsubishi Mirage	919	No
Nissan 240SX	407	No
Nissan Altima	610	Yes
Nissan Maxima	818	Yes
Olds Eighty-Eight	473	Yes
Plymouth Acclaim	762	Yes
Plymouth Bonneville	359	Yes
Pontiac Trans Sport van	761	No
Saturn SL	705	Yes
Toyota Camry	390	Yes
Toyota Celica	834	Yes
Toyota Corolla	522	Yes
Toyota Previa van	711	Yes
Volkswagen Passat	1,182	No
Volvo 240	282	Yes

Source: National Highway Traffic Safety Administration.
Thanks to Dorothy Brown, St. Joseph's High School, Hammonton, NJ, for suggesting these data.

Does it look to you like cars that come equipped with air bags are safer for the driver? We will make box plots of the data so that we can better compare the scores for cars with air bags to cars without. The following instructions will teach you how to make a box plot of the driver injury scores for the 17 cars with no air bags.

First, list the numbers from smallest to largest. A stem-and-leaf plot may help you do this quickly.

407 520 541 585 696 761 770 772 779 860 870 880 919 919 1,024 1,182 2,065

Second, find the median score.

There are seventeen numbers, thus the median will be the ninth score or 779.

Third, find the median of the lower half.

There are eight cars below the median. The median of their eight scores is the average of the fourth and fifth scores. The average of 585 and 696 is 640.5. The number 640.5 is the lower quartile.

Fourth, find the median of the upper half.

There are eight cars above the median. The median of their eighth scores is the average of 919 and 919. The number 919 is the upper quartile.

Fifth, find the extremes.

The lowest score is 407 and the highest is 2,065.

Sixth, mark dots for the median, quartiles, and extremes below a number line.

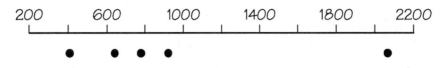

Seventh, draw a box between the two quartiles. Mark the median with a line across the box. Draw two "whiskers" from the quartiles to the extremes.

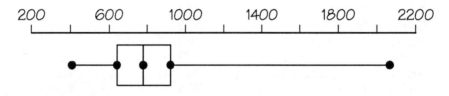

Discussion Questions

1. About what percentage of the cars are
   a. below the median?
   b. below the lower quartile?
   c. above the lower quartile?
   d. in the box?
   e. in each whisker?

2. One whisker is longer than the other. What does this mean?

3. Will the median always be in the center of the box?

4. Using the $1.5 \times$ IQR rule, show that the Chevrolet Astro Van's score of 2,065 is an outlier.

5. The box plot above can be modified to show this outlier. First, copy the box plot above but stop the upper whisker at the Volkswagen Passat's 1,182. Then, put an asterisk at the Astro Van's 2,065.

6. When we find an outlier, it is important to investigate whether the data value might be a mistake or whether the data value represents something that is different in nature from the others. Does anyone in your class have an idea about which is the case here?

7. Which of the two box plots do you think gives a better picture of these data? Why?

   In the following graph, the box plot of the scores for the cars with air bags has been placed below the box plot of the scores for cars without air bags.

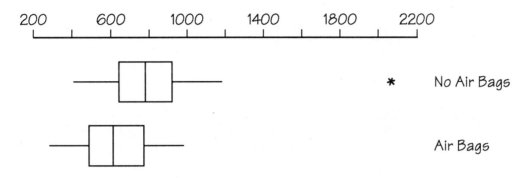

8. Which type of car—those with air bags or those without—is generally safer for the driver? Can you think of reasons other than the air bags why these cars might be safer?

9. Describe the extent of the overlap between the two groups of cars. To get a car that is relatively safe for the driver, is it necessary to get a car with air bags?

10. Write a short essay telling what you have learned about whether or not cars that come equipped with air bags are safer for the driver.

A box plot gives us an easy way to estimate whether or not the data contain outliers. In the box plot of driver injury scores following the seventh step, the length of the box is $919 - 641 = 278$. This is the same as the interquartile range. So $1.5 \times$ IQR would be one-and-a-half box lengths. To estimate if there are any outliers, visually add one-and-a-half box lengths to each end of the box. Any data points beyond those lengths are outliers. Here's how it would look with the box plot from the seventh step.

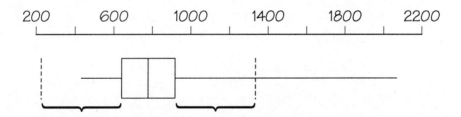

Since the upper whisker goes beyond one-and-a-half box lengths above the upper end of the box, there is at least one outlier in that whisker.

Three box plots are shown below in questions 11, 12 and 13. Estimate whether or not there are any outliers in

a. the upper whisker

b. the lower whisker

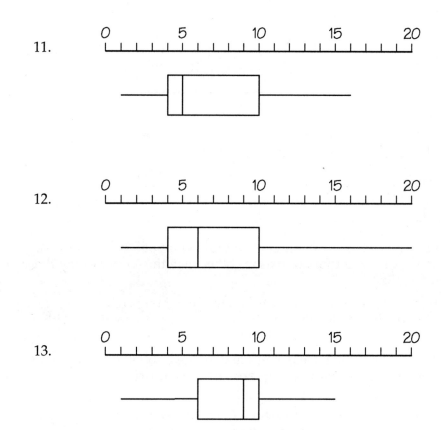

Application 15

Still in School in Fourth Grade

Box plots are most effective when comparing the location and spread of several large sets of data.

The United Nations tries to collect information for each country about living conditions and education. For example, the box plots below show the percentage for various countries of children who enrolled in school in 1985 who are still in school in fourth grade. The box plot for South and Central America is missing. You will add it later.

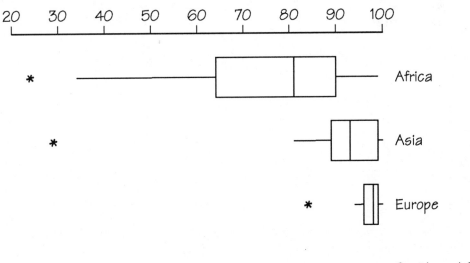

1. The outlier in Asia is Bangladesh. What percentage of children who enroll in school reach fourth grade in Bangladesh?

2. In Egypt, 99% of the children who enroll in school are still in school in fourth grade. Locate Egypt on the box plots above.

3. The United States is not represented in any box plot above. What percentage of children who enroll in school in the United States do you think reach fourth grade?

4. What is the median percentage in Africa?

5. Complete this sentence: In over half of the countries of Asia, at least _____ of the children who enroll in school reach fourth grade.

6. Complete this sentence: In _____ of the countries of Africa, at least 64% of the children who enroll in school reach fourth grade.

Here is a list of the countries of South and Central America, including Mexico, for which data are available on the percentage of children who enroll in school who reach fourth grade.

Country	Percentage	Country	Percentage
Brazil	47%	Mexico	80%
Chile	97	Nicaragua	51
Columbia	62	Panama	87
Costa Rica	87	Paraguay	70
Ecuador	71	Peru	81
El Salvador	57	Surinam	83
Guatemala	46	Uruguay	94
Guyana	97	Venezuela	85
Honduras	55		

Source: The 1993 *Information Please Almanac.*

7. Make a box plot of the percentages for South and Central America. Below the same number line, copy the box plots for the other regions of the world.

8. Write a short essay comparing the percentages for the various parts of the world.

Application 16

Ages of U.S. Vice-Presidents

The following box plot shows the ages of the 20 twentieth-century vice-presidents at their inaugurations.

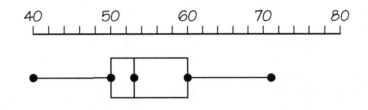

1. The youngest vice-president was Richard Nixon. How old was he at his inauguration?

2. The oldest vice-president at inauguration was Alben William Barkley (Truman's V.P.) How old was he at his inauguration?

3. What was the median age at inauguration?

4. What percentage of the vice-presidents were over 60 (the upper quartile)?

5. What percentage of the vice-presidents were younger than 50 (the lower quartile)?

6. Al Gore was 44 at his inauguration. Complete this sentence: There were at least _____ vice-presidents who were older at the time of their inaugurations.

7. Are any of the vice-presidents outliers? How can you tell?

The following table gives the ages of the 17 twentieth-century presidents at the time they took office.

President	Age at Inauguration
T. Roosevelt	42
Taft	51
Wilson	56
Harding	55
Coolidge	51
Hoover	54
F. Roosevelt	51
Truman	60
Eisenhower	62
Kennedy	43
Johnson	55
Nixon	56
Ford	61
Carter	52
Reagan	69
Bush	64
Clinton	46

8. Make a box plot of the ages of the presidents. Below the same number line, copy the box plot of the ages of the vice-presidents.

9. Write a short essay comparing the ages of the twentieth-century presidents and vice-presidents. Include a sentence about how old a person must be to become president or vice-president of the United States. What is the age limit and where is it found in the U.S. Constitution?

Application 17

Ages of Academy Award Winners

Every year since 1928, an Academy Award has been given to the best actor in a motion picture and to the best actress in a motion picture. The box plots show the ages at which the 67 best actors and 67 best actresses won their Oscars.

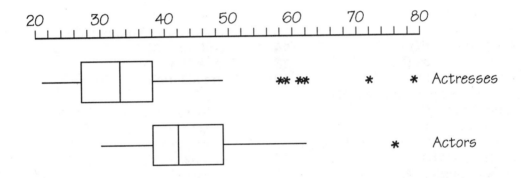

Idea and data courtesy of Gretchen Davis, Santa Monica High School, Santa Monica, CA.

1. How old was the youngest actress (Marlee Matlin) ever to win the award?

2. How old was the youngest actor (a tie between Marlon Brando and Richard Dreyfuss) ever to win the award?

3. What percentage of actors were over age 38? What percentage of actresses were over age 38?

4. The actor whose age was an outlier was Henry Fonda. How old was he when he won?

5. Do actors or actresses have the larger interquartile range?

6. Write a paragraph that describes what you have learned about the ages of the actors and actresses.

Application 18

Sugar in Cereals

Grams of Sugar in a 1-ounce Serving
(rounded to nearest gram)

Cereal	Grams Sugar	Cereal	Grams Sugar
Golden Crisp (K)	15	Cracklin' Oat Bran (A)	7
Smacks (K)	15	Frosted Mini-Wheats (A?)	7
Apple Jacks (K)	14	Just Right (A)	7
Cocoa Pebbles (K)	13	Grape-Nuts (A)	6
Cocoa Puffs (K)	13	Honey Bunches of Oats (A)	6
Cookie Crisp, chocolate (K)	13	Life (K)	6
Froot Loops (K)	13	Multi-Grain Cheerios (A)	6
Cap'n Crunch (K)	12	Quaker Oat Squares (K)	6
Cap'n Crunch, crunch berries (K)	12	Raisin Squares (A)	6
Corn Pops (K)	12	Mueslex Golden Crunch (A)	6
Fruity Pebbles (K)	12	All-Bran (A)	5
Trix (K)	12	Bran Flakes (A)	5
Alpha Bits (K)	11	Grape-Nuts Flakes (A)	5
Cinnamon Mini Buns (A)	11	Post Raisin Bran (A)	5
Cocoa Krispies (K)	11	Quaker Oat Bran (A)	5
Frosted Flakes (K)	11	Team Flakes (A)	5
Honey-Comb (K)	11	Total (A)	5
Apple Cinnamon Cheerios (A)	10	Fruit & Fiber date (A)	5
Peanut Butter Crunch (K)	10	Corn Chex (A)	3
Golden Grahams (A)	10	Crispix (A)	3
Honey Nut Cheerios (K)	10	Product 19 (A)	3
Oatmeal Crisp with Raisins (A)	9	Kix (A)	3
Cinnamon Toast Crunch (K)	9	Rice Krispies (K)	3
Frosted Bran (A)	9	Special K (A)	3
Nut & Honey Crunch (A)	9	Wheat Chex (K)	3
Kellogg's Raisin Bran (K)	9	Wheaties (A?)	3
Double Dip Crunch (A)	8	Corn Flakes (A)	2
Life, cinnamon (K)	8	Nutri•Grain Golden Wheat (A)	2
Wheaties Honey Gold (A)	8	Rice Chex (A)	2
Kellogg's Low Fat Granola (A)	8	Cheerios (A)	1
Fruitful Bran (A)	7	Puffed Rice (A)	0
		Shredded Wheat (A)	0

1. One ounce is approximately 28.4 grams. What percentage of the weight of a box of Smacks is sugar?

2. A teaspoon of sugar weighs about 4 grams. How many teaspoons of sugar are in a 1-ounce serving of Smacks?

We divided the list into "kid" and "adult" cereals as indicated by a (K) or an (A) following each name. If the cereal box had a cartoon character, a child's toy, or a picture of children on the front, we classified it as a kid's cereal (K). Otherwise, the cereal was classified as an adult cereal (A). We were a bit undecided about the two with sports stars on the box (Frosted Mini Wheats and Wheaties), but went with an (A). You may decide to change these.

3. Pick your favorite cereal from the list above. If you eat a 1-ounce serving of your favorite cereal every morning for a year, how many grams of sugar would you eat? How many pounds of sugar? (One pound is about 454 grams.)

4. What is the median number of grams of sugar in all 63 types of cereal?

5. What is the lower quartile?
   What is the upper quartile?

6. Are any of the cereals outliers?

7. Make a box plot of the number of grams of sugar in all 63 types of cereal.

8. Twenty-five of the cereals are classified "kid" cereals; that is, the front of the box had a cartoon character, a child's toy, or children on it. Answer the following questions for those 25 "kid" cereals.

   a. Find the lower extreme.

   b. Find the upper extreme.

   c. Find the median.

   d. Find the lower quartile.

   e. Find the upper quartile.

   f. Are any of the cereals outliers?

   g. Make a box plot of the number of grams of sugar in the "kid" cereals.

9. Thirty-eight of the cereals are classified "adult." Answer these questions for those 38 cereals.

   a. Find the lower extreme.

   b. Find the upper extreme.

   c. Find the median.

   d. Find the lower quartile.

   e. Find the upper quartile.

   f. Are any of the cereals outliers?

   g. Make a box plot of the number of grams of sugar in the "adult" cereals. Put this box plot below the same number line as the box plot for the "kid" cereals.

10. Write a paragraph comparing the number of grams of sugar in a 1-ounce serving of "kid" cereals with the number of grams in "adult" cereals. Discuss why you think there is a difference.

Application 19

World Fertility Rates

The total fertility rate for a country is the average number of children that will be born to a woman, if current fertility rates continue. In other words, the total fertility rate is approximately the total number of children an average woman will give birth to in her lifetime. The fertility rate for the United States is now almost 2.1. The United Nations prepares these estimates every two years.

Below are box plots of the total fertility rate for the countries in various regions of the world, as given by the United Nations in 1993.

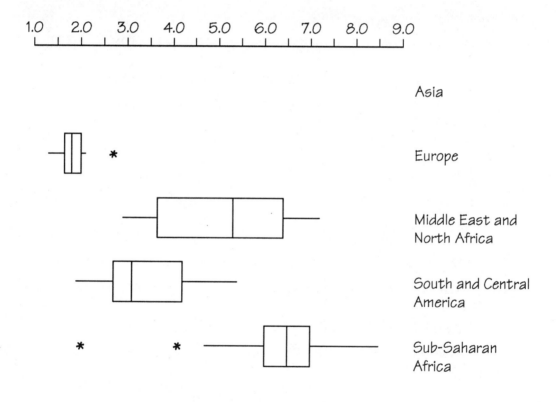

1. The box plot for Asian countries is missing. The data for 22 Asian countries appear below. Add a box plot for the Asian countries to a photocopy or hand-drawn copy of the chart above. Note that the countries below are not listed in order of increasing fertility rate, so you will have to order the data first.

Country	Fertility Rate
Bangladesh	4.7
Bhutan	5.9
Cambodia	4.5
China	2.2
Hong Kong	1.4
India	3.9
Indonesia	3.1
Iran	6.0
Japan	1.7
Laos	6.7
Malaysia	3.6
Mongolia	4.6
Myanmar	4.2
Nepal	5.5
North Korea	2.4
Pakistan	6.2
Philippines	3.9
Singapore	1.7
South Korea	1.8
Sri Lanka	2.5
Thailand	2.2
Vietnam	3.9

Source: United Nations, *The State of World Population,* 1993.

2. The only outliers are Albania in Europe and Mauritius and South Africa in Sub-Saharan Africa. Are these countries different from others in their region?

3. If no children die, what fertility rate means the country will neither decrease nor increase in population? What reasons could explain the fact that the population of Canada, with a fertility rate of 1.8, is increasing?

4. In what region of the world do the countries tend to have the highest fertility rate?

5. Write a paragraph giving an overall summary of the plots.

6. Divide the list of Asian countries in some way that interests you (for example, more developed/less developed) and make a back-to-back stem-and-leaf plot of the two categories. (There will not be enough countries in each category to justify a box plot.) Describe what you have learned.

Possible project: Investigate the reasons for the difference in fertility rates for the various regions of the world. What effect does a high fertility rate have on a country? What effect does a low fertility rate have on a country? Is the infant mortality rate related to the fertility rate? You can get the fertility rates and infant mortality rates for individual countries in many almanacs or from the United Nations. How does the United Nations collect these data?

The Use of Box Plots

It is becoming more and more common to use a box plot to show people how their score compares to other scores. For example, students sometimes take tests to see how interested they are in various occupations. The results from one such test are reproduced below.

BASIC INTEREST SCALES

NATURE	33	V-LOW	
ADVENTURE	55	MOD-H	
MILITARY ACTIVITIES	41	V-LOW	
MECHANICAL ACTIVITIES	40	AVER.	
SCIENCE	36	LOW	
MATHEMATICS	59	HIGH	
MEDICAL SCIENCE	34	LOW	
MEDICAL SERVICE	43	MOD-L	
MUSIC/DRAMATICS	29	V-LOW	
ART	32	V-LOW	
WRITING	26	V-LOW	
TEACHING	28	V-LOW	
SOCIAL SERVICE	43	MOD-L	
ATHLETICS	52	AVER.	
DOMESTIC ARTS	41	LOW	
RELIGIOUS ACTIVITIES	48	AVER.	
PUBLIC SPEAKING	37	MOD-L	
LAW/POLITICS	33	LOW	
MERCHANDISING	45	AVER.	
SALES	46	AVER.	
BUSINESS MANAGEMENT	40	MOD-L	
OFFICE PRACTICES	55	AVER.	

78

Let's examine the "Nature" result more carefully. There are two box plots for "Nature." The top one is for girls and the bottom one is for boys. The top box plot shows that the median interest score in nature for girls is about 51. (The scale is above "Mechanical Activities.") The score of the girl who took the test is marked on each scale by a ∗. Thus, her interest in nature is very low compared to other girls who have taken the test previously.

Discussion Questions

1. For which subject(s) is this girl's interest score in the top 25% of all girls?

2. For which subjects is this girl's interest lowest?

3. Which subjects are girls much more interested in than are boys?

4. Which subjects are boys much more interested in than are girls?

5. Write a letter to this girl recommending possible career choices.

The following plot gives the mathematics proficiency scores for eighth graders on the last National Assessment of Educational Progress. The box plots are a bit different from the ones you have made. The "whiskers" are the lightly-shaded ends of the boxes. In addition, the whiskers do not extend to the lowest score in each state. Before the whiskers were drawn, the top 5% of the scores were eliminated and the bottom 5% of the scores were eliminated.

Distribution of Overall Mathematics Proficiency Organized by Average Proficiency, 1992, Grade 8

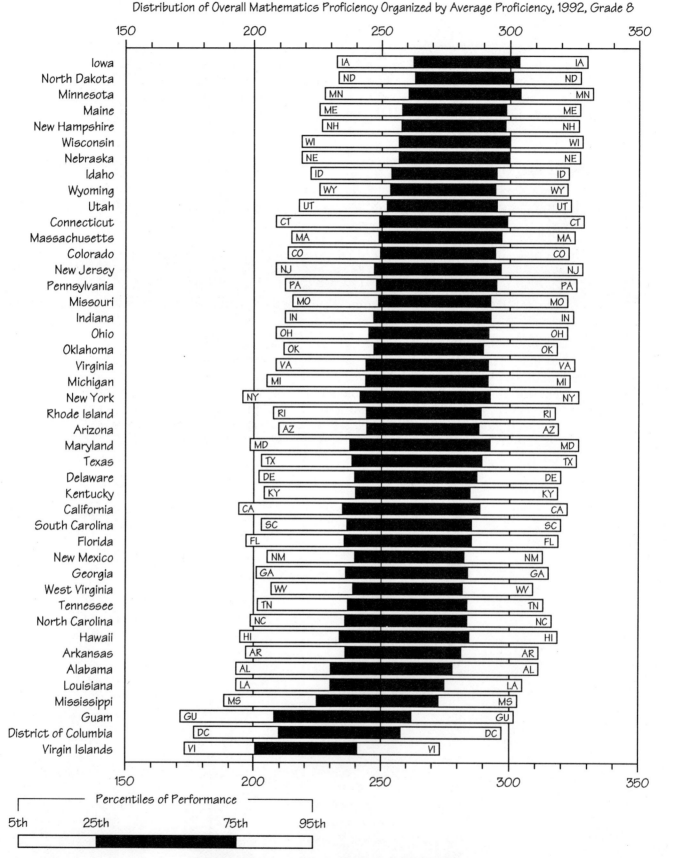

Source: *National Assessment of Educational Progress,
1992 Mathematics Report Card for the Nation and States.*

Discussion Questions

1. Which part of the country had the highest scores? Which part of the country tended to have the lowest scores?

2. In which state was there the most variation in the scores? In which state was there the least variation in the scores?

3. Describe the overlap between the scores of the lowest state, Mississippi, and the scores of the highest state, Iowa.

4. Did the scores vary more between the states or within a typical state?

5. If the box plots had included all scores for each state instead of eliminating the top and bottom scores, how far do you think the whiskers would have extended? Why do you think the top 5% of the scores and the bottom 5% of the scores were eliminated before drawing the box plots?

6. Why did the authors of the report choose to use box plots to display their data?

Box Plots — Summary

You may have found it difficult to see the advantages of using box plots. Some students question the fact that most of the data disappears and only five summary numbers (the median, quartiles, and extremes) remain. It is true that we can no longer spot clusters and gaps, nor can we identify the shape of the distribution as clearly as with number line plots or stem-and-leaf plots. However, we are able to focus on the relative positions of different sets of data and thereby compare them more easily.

Box plots are especially useful when the set of data contains hundreds or even thousands of numbers. A number line plot or stem-and-leaf plot would be unwieldy with thousands of numbers on it! You would not usually make a box plot for a data set with 15 or fewer values. A stem-and-leaf plot would be more appropriate in this case.

To compare two (or more) sets of data using box plots, first look at the boxes to get an idea whether or not they are located in about the same place. Also, study their lengths to determine whether or not the variabilities in the data sets are about the same. Then you can focus on details. Check whether or not one data set has median, upper and lower quartiles, and extremes that are all larger than the corresponding values in the second data set. If it does, then the data in the first set tend to be larger than those in the second no matter which criterion we use for comparing them. If it does not, then there is more uncertainty about which data set is larger. In either case, the plot has helped us learn some details about the similarities and differences between the two data sets. Also, check to see if the pattern of outliers is the same in both data sets.

Notice that even if two (or more) sets of data have unequal numbers of values, this does not cause problems for making comparisons with box plots. This was not true for stem-and-leaf plots.

Suggestions for Student Projects

1. Collect some data on a topic that interests you, construct box plots, and interpret them. Topics that other students have used include:

   - number of hours students work per week

   - number of hours of television watched per week by different types of students

   - allowances of girls and of boys in your class

   - number of times per minute two different groups of people say "like" in ordinary conversation

   - Nielsen ratings for the television shows of the four networks—ABC, CBS, NBC, and FOX. This information is printed weekly in many newspapers. Make four box plots under the same number line.

2. One variation of box plots involves changing the width in proportion to the number of data values represented. For example, if a box representing 100 values is 1 cm wide, then a box representing 50 values would be 0.5 cm wide and a box representing 200 values would be 2 cm wide. Make box plots under the same number line for the adult cereals and kid cereals from Application 18. Make the width of the box proportional to the number of cereals represented. Discuss the merit of this variation.

VI. REVIEW OF ONE-VARIABLE TECHNIQUES

Which Method to Use?

This section is different from the previous five. Each of the previous five introduced some statistical method that can help to interpret data. Then the method was used on several examples. Often more than one of these methods *could* have been used to display and to help interpret a particular set of data. This section helps you choose an appropriate method by giving some comparisons between them.

Before using any statistical method, it is a good idea to ask yourself a few basic questions about the data. How were the numbers obtained? Are the values plausible? What would you like to learn from the data? Do you need the answers to any specific questions? The purpose of statistical methods is to help us learn something useful or interesting from the data, so it is a good idea to keep questions such as these in mind throughout the analysis.

Suppose we have the starting weekly wage for 23 different jobs. We could display the values using a number line plot (Section I), a dot plot (Section II), a stem-and-leaf plot (Section III), or a box plot (Section V). We could calculate statistics such as the median, mean, range, and interquartile range (Section IV). Which of these methods should we use, or, at least, which should we use first? There is no single, correct answer. However, there are some guidelines that can help you to make an appropriate choice of methods.

A reasonable general strategy is to use the simpler methods first. Then, if the interpretations of the data are very clear, there is no need to go on to more complicated displays and methods.

One Group and One Variable

Consider the above example of the starting wage for several jobs. In this example there is one *variable*, the wage. We can treat the various jobs as forming one *group* of jobs. Thus, we have measurements for *one group on one variable*. This is the simplest type of problem for which statistical methods and displays are needed. Most of the examples in Sections I, II, III, and IV are this type of problem.

The number line plot, the dot plot, the stem-and-leaf plot, and the box plot are three different displays that can be used for the one-group/one-variable situation. The following paragraphs describe their relative advantages and disadvantages.

> *Number Line Plot*. The number line plot is easy to construct and interpret. It gives a clear graphical picture, and a few values can be labeled easily. Constructing a number line plot is also a useful first step for calculating the median, extremes, and quartiles. These statements are all true providing the number of values is not too large—fewer than about 25. As the number of values becomes larger, the number line plot can become unwieldy and more difficult to interpret. When a specific value is repeated several times or when there are many nearby values, the number line plot can also become jumbled. Another disadvantage is that it is hard to read the exact

83

numerical values from the number line plot. In conclusion, the number line plot is a useful first display for the one-group/one-variable situation, providing there are about 25 or fewer values in the data.

Dot Plot. The dot plot can be used when you want the label of each data point to be displayed on the graph. By placing all labels and scales on the outside of the box, the data stand out clearly. Given the amount of information conveyed, the dot plot appears remarkably uncluttered, although it takes more space than a number line plot. Like number line plots, dot plots are best used when the number of values is not too large. Repeated values are not a problem with dot plots. One can be listed right below the other.

The dot plot can be used in the same situations as bar graphs. However, the dot plot is more flexible than bar graphs and should be used to display data where there is no natural zero or where it is awkward to include it on the plot. By continuing the light line from one side of the box to the other, the reader will not be tempted to compare the relative lengths of the bars.

Stem-and-Leaf Plot. The stem-and-leaf plot shares many advantages of the number line plot. It is easy to construct and interpret, values can be labeled, and it is a useful first step for calculating the median, extremes, and quartiles. In addition, exact numerical values can be read from the stem-and-leaf plot and repeated values and nearby values in the data cause no special problems. Stem-and-leaf plots do not get as unwieldy as number line plots and dot plots when the number of data values becomes large. On the other hand, a disadvantage is that to construct the stem-and-leaf plot you may have to decide whether to truncate or to round the values. Further disadvantages are the need to decide which values to use for the stems and how to spread out the plot. Thus, it may take more thought to construct the stem-and-leaf plot than the number line plot. The stem-and-leaf plot can display more values than the line plot and dot plot without becoming too confusing in appearance. However, it also has a limit to the number of values that is *reasonable* to display. With more than about 100 values, you will most likely spread out the stem-and-leaf plot. Then it can be useful for up to about 250 values. Above 250, it will be too large and jumbled to interpret easily. In conclusion, for the one-group/one-variable situation with about 25 or fewer values, the stem-and-leaf plot, the number line plot, or the dot plot is a reasonable first display. With about 25 to 250 data values, the stem-and-leaf plot is the most useful first display.

Box Plot. The box plot is more complicated to construct, since you must calculate the median, extremes, and quartiles first. Generally, the simplest way to do this is to construct the stem-and-leaf plot first, and then count in from the ends to get the quartiles and median. Unlike the stem-and-leaf plot, once the box plot is constructed, specific data values cannot be read from it (except for outliers and the median, quartiles, and extremes). The main advantage of the box plot is that it is not cluttered by showing all the data values. It highlights only a few *important* features of the data. Thus, the box plot makes it easier to focus attention on the median, extremes, and quartiles and comparisons among them. Another advantage of the box plot is that it does not become more complicated with more data values. It is useful with any large number of values. The box plot should be avoided when there are only a few data values—fewer than about 15. Then the plotted values might change greatly if only one or a few of the observations were changed.

The box plot is a *summary display* since it shows only certain statistics, not all the data. In conclusion, the box plot is not as useful as the number line, dot, or stem-and-leaf plots for showing details, but it enables us to focus more easily on the median, extremes, and quartiles. Since the number line and stem-and-leaf plots are useful for computing the statistics needed to construct the box plot, it is generally reasonable to make one of these two plots first even if you will eventually construct and use the box plot.

Several Groups and One Variable

Think again about the starting weekly wage example mentioned at the beginning of this section. Instead of considering the 23 jobs as *one group* of jobs, we could divide them into those jobs that require a high school diploma and those that require a college diploma. The jobs are divided into *two groups*. We want to compare the various salaries in these two groups. This is an example of the *two-group/one-variable* problem. Many of the examples in Sections III and V are this type. The following paragraphs describe the relative advantages and disadvantages of the number line, stem-and-leaf, and box plots for this situation.

Number line plots can be placed one above the other to compare two groups, although we did not give any examples of this type.

Back-to-back stem-and-leaf plots are more useful for comparing two groups. They are easy to construct. Comparisons can be made by judging the number of leaves for various stems. However, if the number of data values in the two groups is not roughly equal, the comparisons get more difficult. The details shown in the stem-and-leaf plots can become an obstacle. Furthermore, as the number of values becomes large these plots become unwieldy. For comparing two groups of about equal size with around 100 or fewer data values in each group, back-to-back stem-and-leaf plots are easy to construct and generally adequate.

Box plots below the same number line can also be used to compare two groups. This gives the easiest and most direct comparisons of the outliers, the two minimums, the two lower quartiles, the two medians, the two upper quartiles, and the two maximums. Of course, this does not show any other details, but these quantities are usually sufficient for comparing two groups. Moreover, there are no special problems caused by having a large number of data values, or by having a different number of values in the two groups.

Often, we need to compare more than two groups. For example, the jobs could be broken down into those not requiring a high school diploma, those requiring a high school diploma, those requiring a college degree, and those requiring a graduate degree. This gives four groups. It is an example of a *many-group/one-variable* problem.

There is no way to construct a stem-and-leaf plot for this situation. Several number line plots placed one above the other can be useful if there are not many data values. Box plots are the best choice. The reasons are the same as those given for comparing two groups.

A more concise way to compare two groups than any of these is simply to calculate a single number, such as the mean or median, for each group. But this number hides all the other information in the data. It also loses the advantage of graphical displays. For purposes of exploring and interpreting data, any of the graphical displays will be more valuable than calculating just means or medians. If it is necessary to give a single number to summarize the data, and if there is a possibility of even a few outliers, then the median is usually more valuable than the mean.

As a general conclusion, number line plots, dot plots, stem-and-leaf plots, and box plots each have a useful role for exploring various kinds of data sets. Often, it is worthwhile to make more than one plot. There are no hard and fast rules about which plot should be used, but the previous comparisons can help you make good choices.

The following applications will help you compare the different methods.

Application 20

Letter Frequencies

The number of occurrences of each letter was counted in a very large amount of written material. The percentage that each letter occurred is given in the table below.

A	8.2	J	0.1	S	6.0
B	1.4	K	0.4	T	10.5
C	2.8	L	3.4	U	2.5
D	3.8	M	2.5	V	0.9
E	13.0	N	7.0	W	1.5
F	3.0	O	8.0	X	0.2
G	2.0	P	2.0	Y	2.0
H	5.3	Q	0.1	Z	0.07
I	6.5	R	6.8		

Source: National Council of Teachers of Mathematics.

1. What is the most-used letter?

2. What is the least-used letter?

3. How many *t*'s would you expect to find in a paragraph of 100 letters? In a paragraph of 500 letters?

4. As a group, vowels account for what percentage of letters used?

5. Make a number line plot of the percentages.

6. Make a dot plot of the percentages.

7. Make a stem-and-leaf plot of the percentages.

8. Find the median percentage, the quartiles, and any outliers.

9. Make a box plot of the percentages.

10. Which two letters have the most unusual percentages? From which plot is it easiest to find this information?

11. Are most of the letters used rarely or used more frequently? From which plot is it easiest to find this information?

12. Make a back-to-back stem-and-leaf plot of vowels and consonants.

13. Why isn't it appropriate to make one box plot for vowels and another for consonants?

14. What conclusions can you make by looking at the stem-and-leaf plot you constructed for question 12?

Application 21

Salaries

The table below lists the median weekly salaries of workers employed full time. For example, the median salary for carpenters is $425 because half of the carpenters earn less than $425 and half earn more than $425.

Occupation	Median Weekly Earnings	Occupation	Median Weekly Earnings
Architect	$623	Librarian	$521
Auto mechanic	385	Machinist	476
Bank teller	281	Mail carriers	580
Bartender	249	Mechanical engineer	836
Bookkeeper	345	Newspaper reporter, editor	593
Carpenter	425	Office machine repairperson	468
Cashier	218	Personnel manager	752
Chemist	687	Physician	984
Child care worker	132	Police officer	595
Clergy	459	Real estate salesperson	517
College teacher	756	Registered nurse	634
Computer programmer	662	Retail sales worker (apparel)	246
Cosmetologist	263	Secretary	359
Economist	732	Sewing machine operator	326
Farm worker	239	Social worker	466
Insurance salesperson	513	Taxi driver	339
Janitor	292	Travel agent	408
K–6 teacher	537	Truck driver (heavy trucks)	429
Lab technician	461	Waiter/Waitress	218
Lawyer	1,008		

Source: United States Bureau of Labor Statistics, 1993.

1. Which kind of worker earns the most?

2. Which kind of worker earns the least?

3. Suppose you want to see how the salary of the occupation you are most interested in compares to the other salaries. Which do you think is best for this use: a number line plot, a dot plot, a stem-and-leaf plot, or a box plot?

4. Construct the plot you selected.

5. In one or two sentences, describe how the salary of the occupation you are most interested in compares to the other salaries.

6. The earnings above are for *salaried* employees. In some of the professions listed above, the typical worker is self-employed, not salaried. Do some research to determine which professions these are. What is the median weekly earnings for these self-employed people?

Application 22

Money Spent Per Student

The values in the table below are the amount of money spent on education per student for each of the 50 states and the District of Columbia.

State	Money Spent per Student	State	Money Spent per Student
Alabama	$3,627	Montana	$5,204
Alaska	8,330	Nebraska	5,038
Arizona	4,309	Nevada	4,653
Arkansas	3,700	New Hampshire	5,672
California	4,491	New Jersey	8,645
Colorado	5,064	New Mexico	3,895
Connecticut	7,602	New York	8,565
Delaware	5,865	North Carolina	4,488
District of Columbia	9,259	North Dakota	4,199
Florida	5,276	Ohio	5,245
Georgia	4,466	Oklahoma	3,791
Hawaii	5,166	Oregon	5,683
Idaho	3,386	Pennsylvania	6,541
Illinois	5,520	Rhode Island	6,343
Indiana	4,930	South Carolina	4,351
Iowa	4,679	South Dakota	3,965
Kansas	4,874	Tennessee	3,782
Kentucky	4,354	Texas	4,438
Louisiana	4,146	Utah	2,960
Maine	5,458	Vermont	6,738
Maryland	6,566	Virginia	4,836
Massachusetts	6,366	Washington	5,000
Michigan	5,883	West Virginia	4,911
Minnesota	5,239	Wisconsin	5,871
Mississippi	3,187	Wyoming	5,723
Missouri	4,754		

Source: National Center for Education Statistics, 1991.

1. Using the value for your state and the number of students in your school, give a rough estimate of the total cost of running your school for a year.

2. Suppose you want to know how your state compares to the others. Construct a plot to help you make this comparison. Then write a paragraph describing the overall distribution of expenses and the relative position of your state.

3. Using the map of the United States on page 29, classify each state as being northern or southern. Then construct a plot to show how the expenses per student compare in the two halves of the country. Write a paragraph summarizing the comparisons.

Possible project: Is the money spent per student related to how successful the schools are? Information about graduation rates and standardized test results may be found in almanacs and publications of the National Center for Education Statistics. Collect some of this information and begin to think about how to answer the question. In the next section, you will learn some techniques that may help you.

Application 23

Alternatives to Pie Charts

Pie charts (sometimes called circle graphs) are often used when comparing parts of a whole. The pie charts below show the racial/ethnic distribution of the United States population in 1970 and 1990.

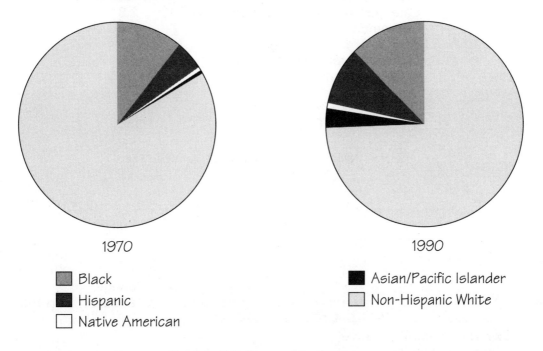

1970   1990

■ Black   ■ Asian/Pacific Islander
■ Hispanic   ☐ Non-Hispanic White
☐ Native American

Source: U.S. Bureau of the Census.

Although they have a rather nifty appearance, pie charts are difficult to comprehend. In order to read a pie chart, you must compare the areas of sectors of a circle. For example, in the pie charts above, it is difficult to see whether there was a higher percentage of Hispanics or of Blacks in 1990. (The respective percentages were 9% and 12%). It is even more difficult to compare percentages in 1970 with those in 1990.

The sets of data below are each of the type that might be displayed on a pie chart. Choose a plot from those you have learned, or invent a new type of plot to display each set of data.

1. Popular vote in the 1992 presidential election:

Bill Clinton	**43%**
George Bush	**38%**
Ross Perot	**19%**
Total	**100%**

2. Occupations eighth-graders expect to have when they are 30:

Professional, business, managerial	28.6%
Military, police, security	9.6
Business owner	6.2
Technical	6.2
Science or engineering professional	5.9
Service worker	4.9
Craftsperson or operator	4.2
Salesperson, clerical, office worker	2.8
Homemaker	2.3
Farmer or farm manager	1.0
Laborer or farm worker	0.6
Other employment	17.0
Don't know	10.5
Total	**100%**

Source: National Center for Education Statistics, 1988.

3. Percentage of high school and college graduates in each job category:

	Education		Median Weekly
	High School Graduate	College Graduate	Earnings
Executive, administrative, and managerial	5%	20%	$670
Professional (incl. teachers engineers, nurses, writers)	2	33	684
Technicians (incl. computer programmers, draftspeople)	2	5	522
Sales	14	14	450
Administrative support (incl. receptionists, secretaries, clerks, teacher's aids)	20	14	392
Service (incl. waiters, janitors, police, dental assistants, hair-dressers)	22	7	292
Farming, forestry, and fishing	3	1	267
Precision product, craft, and repair (incl. mechanics, carpenters, machinists, butchers)	10	3	498
Operators, fabricators, and laborers (incl. truck drivers, sewing machine operators, welders, vehicle washers)	22	4	361

Source: U. S. Bureau of Labor Statistics, *Occupational Outlook Quarterly,* 1993.

VII. SCATTER PLOTS

In the 1992 Summer Olympics, the United States men's basketball team, known as the Dream Team, won the gold medal. After winning all five preliminary games, they entered the single-elimination medal round along with seven other teams. The Dream Team then defeated Puerto Rico, Lithuania, and Croatia by an average score of 120 to 79 to claim the gold medal. The table below gives the cumulative box score for the United States players over these three final games.

United States Dream Team								
	Min	FG-A	FT-A	R	A	S	Pf	Pts
Charles Barkley	48	14-22	4-5	6	7	7	10	36
Larry Bird	47	6-12	4-5	13	7	4	2	17
Clyde Drexler	54	13-21	0-0	7	9	5	5	28
Patrick Ewing	54	14-24	4-9	14	0	2	5	32
"Magic" Johnson	72	15-25	2-4	9	21	6	3	38
Michael Jordan	67	20-45	7-7	9	9	10	7	47
Christian Laettner	17	1-3	11-12	8	2	1	6	14
Karl Malone	45	13-21	10-14	15	2	5	4	36
Chris Mullin	60	16-20	3-4	5	8	2	2	42
Scottie Pippen	56	11-17	2-3	6	14	6	3	26
David Robinson	57	13-20	10-14	17	1	5	3	36
John Stockton	23	3-6	1-1	1	8	0	1	7
Totals	600	139-236	58-78	110	88	53	51	359

Shooting field goals, 58.9%, free throws, 74.3%

Key for Table

Min	Minutes played
FG-A	Field goals made—field goals attempted
FT-A	Free throws made—free throws attempted
R	Rebounds
A	Assists
S	Steals
Pf	Personal fouls
Pts	Total points scored

Discussion Questions

1. How many rebounds did Larry Bird make?

2. Which player played the most minutes?

3. Which player had the most personal fouls?

4. How many field goals did Magic Johnson make? How many did he attempt? What percentage did he make?

5. Five players are on the court at one time for each team, and this table includes three games. Determine how many minutes are in a game.

6. How is the Pts (total points scored) column computed? Verify that this number is correct for Patrick Ewing and for Karl Malone. (Caution: Some of the field goals for other players were three-point shots. How can you determine the number of three-point shots a player made?)

Do you think the players who played the most minutes are generally the players who scored the most points? To find out, scan the Min and Pts columns in the box score. To further investigate this question, we will make a *scatter plot* showing minutes played (Min) and total points scored (Pts). First, set up a plot with minutes played on the horizontal axis and total points scored on the vertical axis.

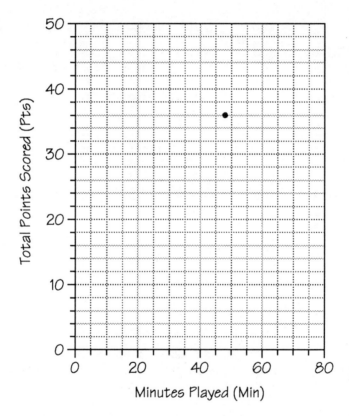

Charles Barkley, the first player, played 48 minutes and scored a total of 36 points in the three games. The • on the preceding plot represents Barkley. The • is above 48 and across from 36.

The completed scatter plot follows.

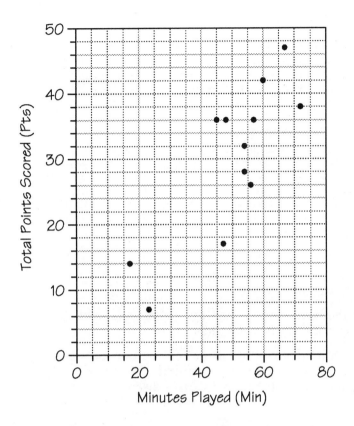

As we suspected, this plot shows that players who played more minutes generally scored more points, and the players who played fewer minutes scored fewer points. Thus, there is a *positive* association between minutes played and points scored.

However, we can see more from this plot. For example, there are two players in a cluster at the lower left of the scatter plot; both of these players played fewer minutes and scored fewer points than the remaining ten players. Yet the points and minutes played for both players seem to follow a relationship similar to the other players; these two players are simply lower on both variables. Referring back to the box score we see that these players are Stockton and Laettner.

In this scatter plot we used • as the plotting symbol. Other common plotting symbols are X, $+$, 0, and $*$. Sometimes informative labels that differ from one point to another, such as the first letter of the player's name, make appropriate plotting symbols.

Discussion Questions

1. Using the scatter plot, find the point that represents the player who scored the most points.

2. Using the scatter plot, did this player also play the most minutes?

3. Using the box score, find the name of the player from question 1. Did he also attempt the most field goals?

4. Use the scatter plot to answer the following question. If a "typical" Dream Team member had played 50 minutes, about how many points would you expect him to have scored?

5. Laettner scored 14 points in 17 minutes. Thus, he scored at a rate of 14/17 = 0.82 points-per-minute. That is, on average he scored about 0.8 points each minute he played. Could he have scored *exactly* 0.8 points during any one minute? What is the smallest number of points he could have scored during a minute? What is the most he could have scored in a minute?

6. Determine the points-per-minute scoring rate for the other player in the cluster at the lower left of the scatter plot. Is this lower or higher than Laettner's rate? Where is his point on the scatter plot compared to Laettner's point?

7. No player scored at a rate as high as one point per minute played. If a player had scored at such a high rate, where in the scatter plot would this point be plotted?

8. For the "typical" Dream Team player using points and minutes from question 4, what is his points-per-minute scoring rate? What was Michael Jordan's scoring rate?

9. Using the scatter plot, identify the players with the highest and lowest points-per-minute scoring rates.

10. Write a brief description of the information conveyed by this scatter plot. Then read the following sample discussion. Did you notice any information not listed in this sample discussion?

In this plot, we were not surprised to see a positive association between the number of minutes played and the total points scored by the members of the Dream Team during their final three Olympic basketball games. The points seem to cluster into two groups: the two players at the lower left played fewer minutes, approximately 20 each, while each of the other ten played 45 minutes or more. However, the players in both groups have about the same relationship between their points scored and minutes played. The two players in the lower group, who are Laettner and Stockton, played less time but were about as effective on a scoring-per-minute-played basis as the others.

Considering the ten players who appeared for 45 minutes or more, one point could be considered an outlier in terms of scoring somewhat less—and at a lower rate—than the others; this point represents Larry Bird. The player who scored the most was Michael Jordan and the one who played the most was Magic Johnson, but their scoring rates (points-per-minute played) were similar to those for the other players.

An assist is a pass that leads directly to a basket. A player is credited with a rebound when he recovers the ball following a missed shot. Do you think players who get a lot of rebounds also make a lot of assists? It is difficult to answer this question just by looking at the box score.

To answer this question, we will make a scatter plot showing rebounds (R) and assists (A).

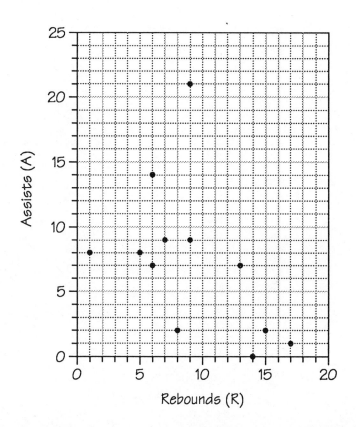

This plot shows that the players who got *more* rebounds generally had *fewer* assists, and players who got *fewer* rebounds had *more* assists. Thus, there is a *negative* association between rebounds and assists. Moreover, the player with 9 rebounds and 21 assists seems to be an outlier. In comparison with the other players, he had many assists for his number of rebounds.

Discussion Questions

1. Who was this player with many assists?

2. Did the players who got the most rebounds also make the most assists?

3. Suppose a player had 10 rebounds. About how many assists would you expect this player to have?

4. Are there any other points in this scatter plot that you would say are outliers? If so, identify them and give your reasons.

5. Why do you suppose players who get a lot of rebounds do not make a lot of assists?

6. If you were the coach and you wanted a player to make more assists, would you instruct him to make fewer rebounds?

The following scatter plot shows assists and total points scored for the Dream Team players.

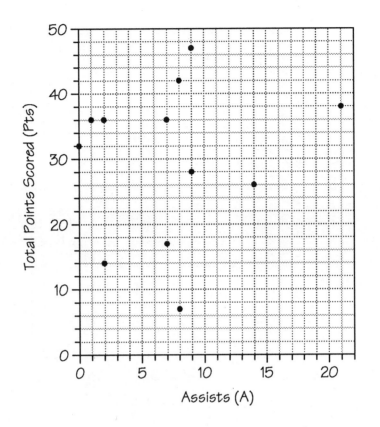

This plot shows *no association* between assists and total points scored. The one outlier on assists, Magic Johnson, scored more points than average, so this point alone could give a hint of slight positive association to the scatter plot. However, if we cover this point with a finger, there is absolutely no indication of positive or negative association among the remaining points. Thus, we say that overall there is no association in this scatter plot.

In summary, the following scatter plots show positive association.

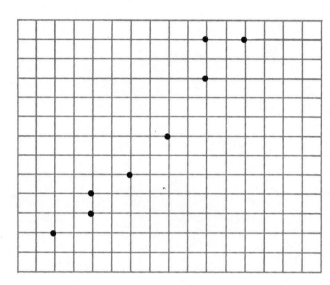
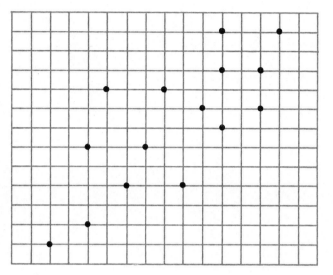

The following scatter plots show negative association.

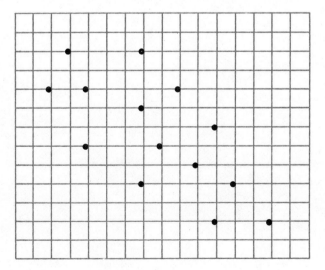
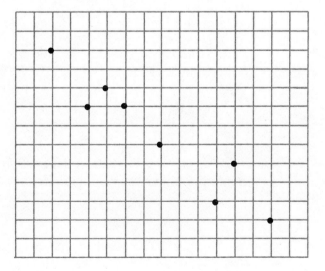

The following scatter plots show no association.

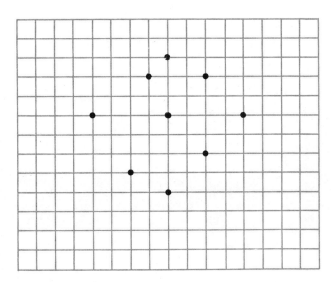 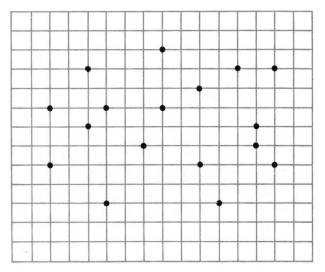

Sometimes one or two points can make it appear that there is a positive or negative association when there is really no association. If you can cover up one or two points and make it look as if there is no association, there probably really is none.

When describing the information displayed on a scatter plot, you can discuss

1. whether there is positive, negative, or no association;

2. whether there are any clusters of points and whether the points in the clusters have anything in common; and

3. whether any points do not follow the general pattern and could be called outliers.

It's not always safe to conclude that one variable *causes* another to happen (or not happen) just because there is an association.

Application 24

Marriage and Divorce

The table below shows marriage and divorce rates (per 1,000 population) for European countries and the United States.

	Marriage Rate (Per 1,000 Population)	Divorce Rate
Austria	5.6	2.0
Denmark	6.0	3.0
Finland	5.1	2.9
France	5.0	1.9
Germany	6.7	2.0
Hungary	6.3	2.4
Italy	5.4	0.4
Netherlands	6.1	1.9
Norway	4.9	2.2
Poland	6.8	1.3
Sweden	5.2	2.2
Switzerland	6.8	2.0
United Kingdom	6.1	2.9
United States	9.7	4.8

Source: United Nations *Demographic Yearbook 1990* and *Monthly Bulletin of Statistics*, June 1991.

Here is the scatter plot of the divorce rate against the marriage rate for these countries.

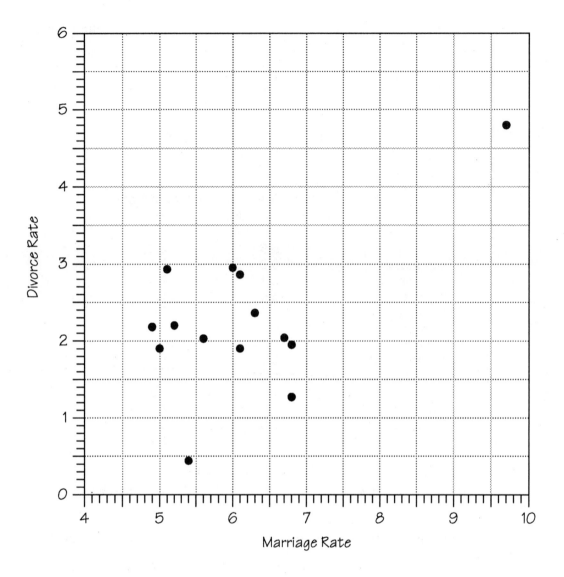

Note that the scale on the horizontal axis extends from 4.0 to 10.0 since this includes all these marriage rates. We did not extend the scale all the way down to 0.0. If we had done so, the scatter plot would have all its points in the right half and the left part would be blank. The points would not fill the plotting space very well, making it harder to see any patterns, clusters, or outliers. Sometimes it is reasonable to include 0.0 in the axis scale, but there is no hard and fast rule telling when to do so.

1. About how many weddings would you expect to occur each year in a U.S. city with population 100,000? each week? What assumptions must be made to produce these estimates?

2. The scatter plot suggests that at least one country is an outlier compared to the others in terms of these rates. Which country is most clearly an outlier?

3. Ignoring this outlier, is there positive association, negative association, or no association between the marriage and divorce rates in the remaining countries?

4. Considering only the European countries, are there any that you would consider outliers in terms of these rates? If so, give its (their) name(s).

5. Luxembourg is a very small European country. Its marriage rate was 5.8. What would you predict for its divorce rate? What is a range of values (an upper value and a lower value) that you would expect its divorce rate to fall between?

6. If a country has a marriage rate of 6.0 per 1,000 population and a divorce rate of 2.0 per 1,000 population, how many divorces would you expect per marriage? Write a sentence describing what this number means. Would it make sense for this number ever to be larger than 1? If so, explain how; if not, explain why not.

7. Calculate the expected number of divorces per marriage in each of these countries, and make a stem-and-leaf plot of these values. Write a description of this information, including whether or not you consider any countries to be outliers in terms of this measure.

8. Write a paragraph summarizing how the marriage and divorce rates for the United States compare to these European countries. Include a discussion of any outliers you identified in questions 2 and 4.

Possible project: Find similar data for countries in some other region of the world (for example, South America or Asia), and compare the United States to these countries.

Protein Versus Fat

The following scatter plot shows the grams of fat against the grams of protein in individual servings of lunch and dinner items sold at a fast-food restaurant.

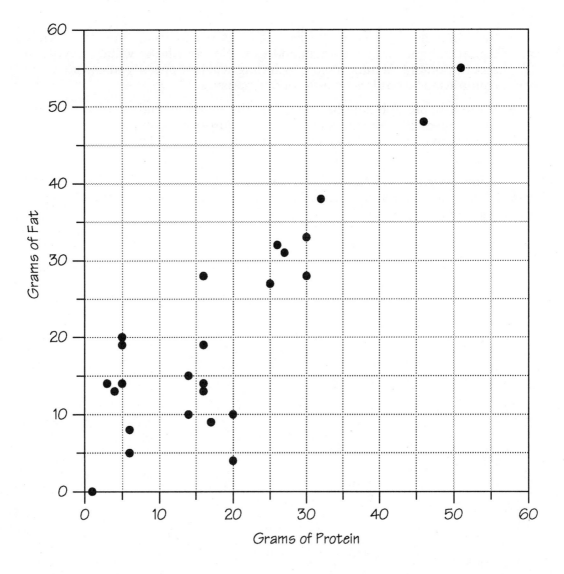

1. What is the largest number of grams of protein in any item?

2. What is the number of grams of fat in the item in question 1?

3. Does the item in question 1 have an unusually large amount of fat considering how much protein it has?

4. What is the smallest number of grams of protein in any item?

5. How many grams of fat does the item in question 4 have?

6. Is there a positive, negative, or no association between grams of protein and grams of fat?

7. If a new item has 30 grams of protein, how many grams of fat would you expect it to have?

8. Suppose you want protein without much fat. Give the number of grams of protein and fat in the item that you would select.

9. Are there any other item(s) that would be almost as good in terms of providing a lot of protein without much fat? Give the number of grams of protein and fat for such item(s).

10. Do you see any clusters of points? Where?

The fast food items used to construct this scatter plot were those given at the beginning of Section III, page 21. Refer back to that table to answer the following questions.

11. What is the item that you decided to order in question 8?

12. If you listed any items for question 9, give their names.

13. Name the items in any cluster you listed for question 10.

14. With the possible exception of an outlier or cluster, are the remaining points scattered fairly closely about a straight line?

15. Write a summary of the information displayed in the scatter plot. Discuss any clusters, outliers, and general relationships you see among these food items.

Application 26

Dual-Deck Cassettes

The following table lists 16 dual-deck model mid-priced cassette decks, each with its price and overall score. *Consumers Union* says that the overall score "reflects both performance in our lab tests and our judgment regarding the presence of useful features. Differences in score of 10 points or less were judged not very significant." Higher scores are better.

Ratings of Dual-Deck Cassettes as Published in the March 1992 issue of *Consumer Reports*

Brand and Model	Price	Overall Score
Sony TC-WR875	$500	88
Sony TC-WR775	285	83
Denon DRW-850	500	82
Kenwood KX-W8030	280	80
Pioneer CT-W850R	380	80
Sansui D-X311WR	280	80
Yamaha KX-W332	375	79
Carver TDR-2400	500	78
JVC TD-W505TN	210	78
Onkyo TA-RW470	370	77
Teac W-580R	250	77
JVC TD-W805TN	380	76
Technics RS-TR555	270	74
Pioneer CT-W550R	250	71
Radio Shack Optimus SCT-89	300	71
Pioneer Elite CT-WM77R	365	70

Source: March 1992 issue of *Consumer Reports*.

1. Which cassette player do you think is the best buy?

2. A scatter plot will give a better picture of the relative price and overall score of these dual-deck cassettes. Make a scatter plot with price on the horizontal axis. When constructing a scatter plot, one of the first things you must do is choose the scales by deciding on the upper and lower limits for both axes. Quickly scan the data and choose limits that are "round" numbers at or slightly beyond the extreme values in the data.

3. These data contain two cassettes with the identical values of (280, 80). Does your scatter plot indicate that there are two such items? What are some alternative ways of displaying this information in the plot?

4. In your scatter plot identify those cassette decks that have a high overall score given their price. Choose one or several, depending on how many you feel stand out as being an especially good value.

5. Write a sentence or two justifying your choice(s) in question 4.

6. Is there a positive, negative, or no association between price and overall score?

7. Given their prices, which cassette decks perform poorly?

SAT Scores

The following plot shows the mean SAT math score in each state against the percentage of high school seniors in that state who took the test. Each state is identified by its postal code. For example, Mississippi is MS. The nationwide mean was 478.

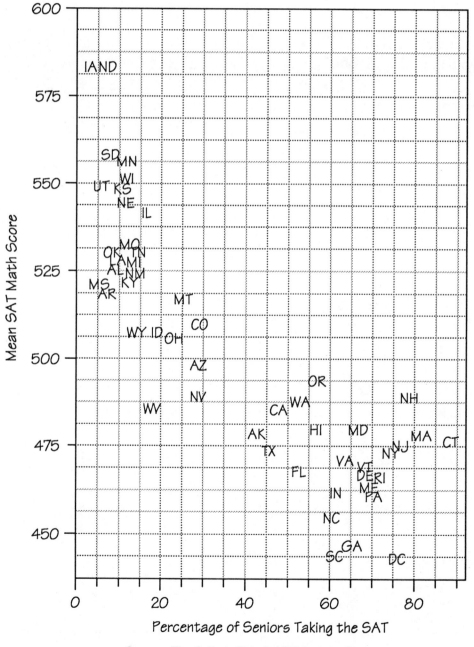

Source: The College Board, 1993 test results.

1. In general, as a larger percentage of students take the test, what happens to the SAT math score?

2. Find the two clusters of states. Within the cluster on the left, is there a positive, negative, or no association between the percentage taking the test and the score?

3. Within the cluster on the right, is there a positive, negative, or no association?

4. Taking into account the percentage of students taking the test, which state(s) do you think have the best SAT math score? Which have the worst?

5. Using the facts you discovered in questions 1 through 4, write a summary of the information given in the scatter plot. Include an analysis of the position of your state.

Scatter Plots — Summary

Scatter plots are the best way to display data in which two numbers are given for each person or item. When you analyze a scatter plot, look for the following:

- positive, negative, or no association
- clusters of points
- points that do not follow the general pattern

If you find any of these features, try to determine what could have caused them.

When you construct a scatter plot, you must decide on the scale to use for each axis. Sometimes, but not always, it makes sense to include 0. You must also decide on the symbols to use as plotting characters. Often using symbols that identify the item, such as a state's two-letter abbreviation, makes interpretation easier. Just be careful that the scatter plot does not become too complicated.

Suggestions for Student Projects

Think of a problem that interests you or select one of those below. Collect the data, make the appropriate plot(s), and write a summary of your results. Try to explain any patterns, clusters, or outliers.

1. Did the students who studied the most hours tend to get the higher grades on your last test?

2. Do students who get the most allowance tend to work more hours doing chores at home?

3. Can the students who do the most sit-ups in one minute also do the most push-ups?

4. Investigate whether there are relationships between certain physical characteristics by measuring a group of students. Some possibilities include the following:

   a. height and elbow-hand length

   b. circumference of closed fist and length of foot

   c. hand span and circumference of wrist

   d. weight and waist

   e. circumferences of head and neck

5. Find two variables that have positive association and it is clear that one variable causes the other. Find two variables that have positive association but one does not cause the other.

VIII. LINES ON SCATTER PLOTS

The y = x Line

In the last section we interpreted scatter plots by looking for general relationships of positive, negative, and no association. We also looked for clusters of points and outliers that seemed special in some way. This section shows how interpretations of scatter plots are helped sometimes by adding a straight line to the plot. Two different straight lines are used. One is the $y = x$ line going through the points (0, 0), (1, 1), (2, 2), and so forth. The second type is a straight line that is placed so that it is close to many data points.

In a study of the interests of early adolescents, both boys and girls were asked to indicate their degree of interest in several subjects by rating each on a seven-point scale, with one meaning low interest and seven high interest. The students were in grades 5 through 9 with ages ranging from 10 to 15, and the mean age was 12.6 for both boys and girls. The data below are means for each group.

Early Adolescent Interests		
Subject	Girls	Boys
Love	6.5	6.4
Life	6.4	6.2
Money	6.3	6.5
People	6.1	5.6
Opposite Sex	6.0	6.2
Music	6.0	5.3
Peace	5.8	5.5
Religion	5.5	5.1
Animals	5.5	5.2
Television	5.3	5.5
Sports	5.2	6.1
Movies	5.2	5.4
Cars	5.0	5.7
School	4.4	3.3
Cooking	4.4	3.1
Teachers	4.3	3.6
Magazines	4.2	4.1
Other countries	3.8	3.6
Generation gap	3.6	3.5
Motorcycles	3.4	5.7
Death	2.3	2.0
War	1.9	3.1
Alcohol	1.7	1.9
Cigarettes	1.7	1.6
Drugs	1.5	1.6

Source: *Journal of Early Adolescence*, Vol. 1, pages 365–372.
Thanks to Chris Olsen, Washington High School, Cedar Rapids, IA for suggesting these data.

Scanning the two columns of data shows that boys and girls generally gave similar ratings to each subject, suggesting a strong positive association between what boys and girls find interesting. We would be surprised if it were otherwise! To investigate additional questions concerning how the interests of boys and girls in these subjects compare, it helps to make a scatter plot from the data. The scatter plot of boys' mean rating against girls' mean rating follows.

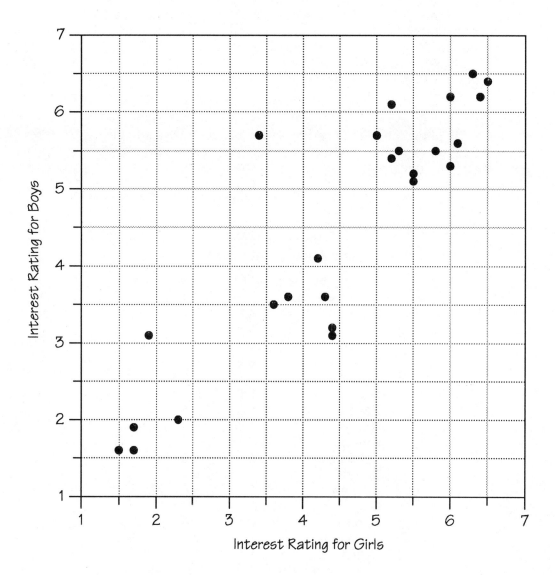

Discussion Questions

1. Does the scatter plot confirm that boys' and girls' interests have strong positive association?

2. Place a ruler on the plot next to the line going through (1,1), (2,2), (3,3), and so forth up to (7,7). If a data point is exactly on this line, what can we say about boys' interests and girls' interests for this subject?

3. Explain why the following statement is true: If a point is above this line, the boys' interest rating for this subject is greater than the girls' interest rating. How many points are above this line? Pick three such points, and for each identify the subject by using the data table.

4. How many points fall below this line? What can we say about these subjects?

5. Identify the two points that are the largest (vertical) distance above this line. What are these subjects? Explain why the vertical distance of any point from this line is the same as the horizontal distance.

6. Consider all 25 points in the scatter plot. How many would you say are "reasonably close" to this line? What can you say about boys' and girls' interests in these subjects? The remaining points therefore must be those that you would consider "not reasonably close" to the line, and some are above it and some are below. Identify the subjects that are above the line but not reasonably close to it. Identify the subjects that are below the line but not reasonably close to it.

7. Notice the cluster of three or four points near the lower left corner of the scatter plot. What can you say about boys' and girls' interests in these subjects? Identify these subjects using the data table. Do you believe these data? Do you think early adolescents really are not interested in these subjects? Do you have another explanation for why these ratings came out the way they did?

8. If you were going to repeat this study using students in your school, what subjects would you add or delete from the list? How would you plan the study so that you could learn, as accurately as possible, boys' and girls' true interests in these subjects?

The following two paragraphs summarize our information.

In this scatter plot representing boys' and girls' interests in 25 subjects, we could say that for about 17 of these subjects the boys' and girls' interests are "reasonably close" to each other, since these points are quite near the $y = x$ line. (More precisely, these mean ratings differ by 0.5 or less.) This group includes the subjects rated of most interest by both boys and girls, which are love, life, money, the opposite sex, and people. It is interesting to consider the subjects where boys and girls differ. The biggest difference is that boys are much more interested in motorcycles than are girls. Boys are also more interested in war, sports, and cars. Girls are more interested in cooking, school, teachers, and music.

We also see that there is a cluster of three subjects in which both pre-adolescent boys and girls report very low interest. These subjects are alcohol, cigarettes, and drugs. One wonders if these data really represent a true result! Perhaps the students' answers were not anonymous, or at least the students believed that their answers were not anonymous, so they might have reported what they felt they were supposed to say, rather than their true interest level. If this were the situation for these three subjects, might it also have occurred with other less controversial topics in the list? We can't say for sure. But understanding how a study was done and knowing exactly how the data were obtained are important parts of drawing accurate conclusions from data.

In this example, both boys and girls rated their interests on a scale from one to seven. Since the scales are the same, the number lines on the x- and y-axes should also be the same. The plot will be square. The points, say, (2,5) and (5,2) will then be symmetric with respect to the $y = x$ line, which is the impression we want to convey.

Some calculators and computer software won't construct a square plot, making one of the points above look farther from the line than the other.

In summary, this $y = x$ line divides the plot into two regions. We should try to distinguish the characteristics of the points in the two regions.

Application 28

Submarine Sinkings

During World War II, the United States Navy tried to estimate how many German submarines were sunk each month. After the war, the Navy was able to get the actual numbers. The results follow:

Month	U.S. Estimate	Actual Number of Sinkings
1	3	3
2	2	2
3	4	6
4	2	3
5	5	4
6	5	3
7	9	11
8	12	9
9	8	10
10	13	16
11	14	13
12	3	5
13	4	6
14	13	19
15	10	15
16	16	15

Source: Mosteller, Fienberg, and Rourke, *Beginning Statistics with Data Analysis*.

1. Make a scatter plot of the data. Put the U.S. estimate on the horizontal axis.

2. Draw in the line that connects all the points where the number estimated by the U.S. Navy would be the same as the actual number of sinkings.

3. If a point is above the line, does it mean that the U.S. Navy's estimate was too high or too low?

4. Are more points above the line or below it?

5. Did the U.S. Navy tend to underestimate or overestimate the number of submarine sinkings?

6. Which point is farthest from the line? How many units away from the line is it? (Count the units vertically from the point to the line.)

7. How many points are three units or more from the line?

Fitting a Line

The Second International Assessment of Educational Progress studied the mathematics and science skills of samples of 9- and 13-year-old students from countries that agreed to participate. The study also collected information on educational and cultural factors that might be associated with student achievement.

The following table gives the average number of days of instruction in the school year and the percent of correct answers on the science test for 13-year-old students in each country in 1991. The science test contained 64 questions on life, physical, earth, and space sciences, as well as the nature of science.

Area	Average Days in School Year	Percent Correct for Science
Canada	188	69%
France	174	69
Hungary	177	73
Ireland	173	63
Israel	215	70
Italy	204	70
Jordan	191	57
Scotland	191	68
Slovenia	190	70
South Korea	222	78
Soviet republics (Russia)	198	71
Spain	188	68
Switzerland	207	74
Taiwan	222	76
United States	178	67

Source: National Center of Education Statistics, *Learning Mathematics and Learning Science*, 1992.

To investigate possible relationships in these data, we start by constructing the following scatter plot of science percent correct against average days in school year.

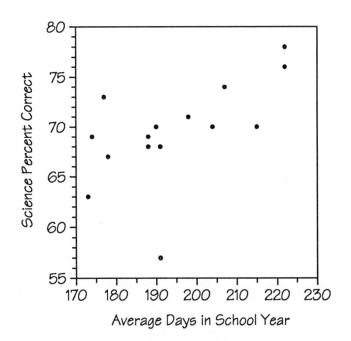

There is a positive association between the variables. For these data, 13-year-old students from countries with a longer school year tended to get a larger percent of the science questions correct.

The same plot with a line through the points follows. This line is called the *fitted line*.

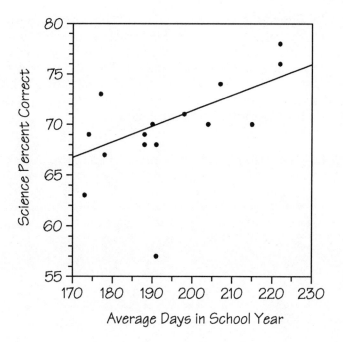

We can use this line to help describe the relationship between these variables. We can also use it for prediction. For example, suppose a country had a 210-day school year. What would you predict for its percent correct?

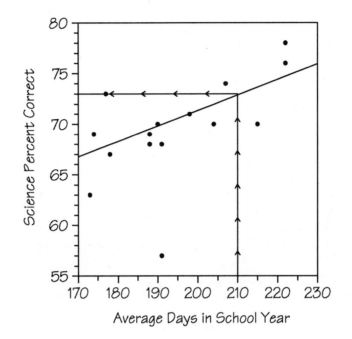

You should expect approximately 73 percent correct.

Now we will describe a method for drawing a line through the data in order to predict percentage correct if we are given days in school year.

First, count the total number of points. Draw two vertical dashed lines so there are approximately the same number of points in each of the three strips.

We have 15 points, so we would like to have five points in each strip. Counting in from the right side, we draw a vertical dashed line separating the right-most five points. Counting in from the left side, however, we see that the fifth and sixth points have exactly the same *x* value. We cannot separate exactly five points; it must be either four or six. In such a situation it is better to have more points in an outer strip rather than in the center strip, so we draw the dashed line separating the outer six points.

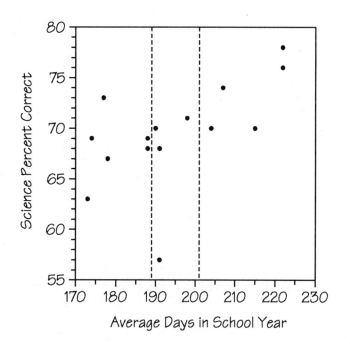

Second, place an X in each strip at the "center" of the points in that strip.

Study the right strip. It has five points. We want to find the median of the days and the median of the percent correct. The median of the days is at the third point counting from the left (or from the right). To find the median of the days, place a ruler to the left of the points and move it toward the right until it is over the third point. Draw a short vertical dashed line there.

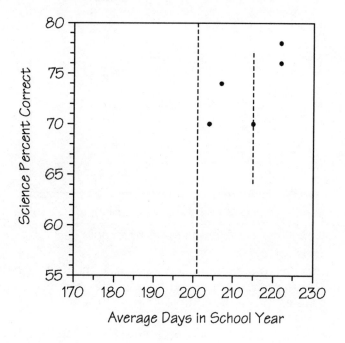

The median of the percent correct is also at the third point, counting from the bottom or top. Move the ruler up until it is over the third point and draw a horizontal dashed line there. The plot is shown as follows:

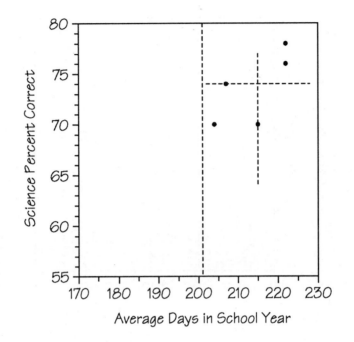

Mark an *X* where the dashed lines cross.

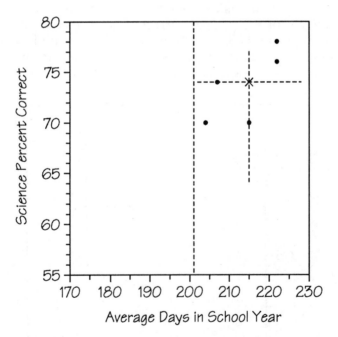

The center strip has four points. The median of the days is halfway between the second and third point, counting from the left or right. Here the days for these two points are equal, so the common value is the median.

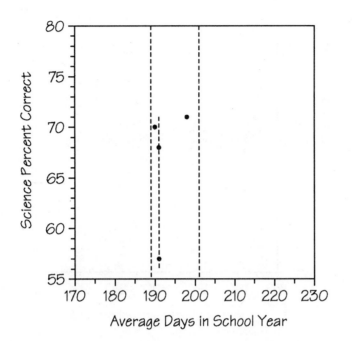

The median of the percentage correct is halfway between the second and third point, counting from the bottom or top.

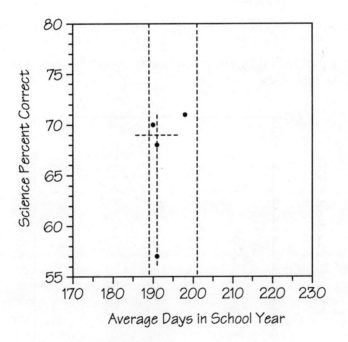

Mark an X where the dashed lines cross.

After the "center" of the left strip is also found, the plot looks like this:

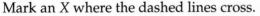

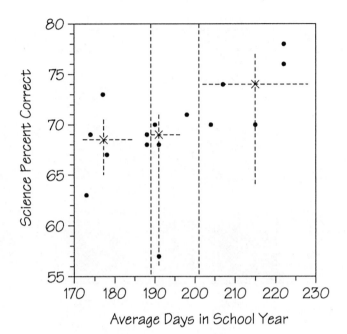

The third step is to decide whether or not the three X's lie close to a straight line. Use your ruler, balanced on its edge, to help decide. For this example, the X's lie approximately on a straight line.

Finally, place your ruler so that it connects the two X's in the outside strips. Now slide the ruler one-third of the way to the middle X and draw the line.

The finished plot including the fitted line is shown below. It is not necessary to include the dashed lines.

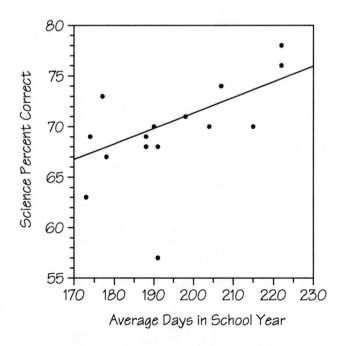

Discussion Questions

1. How many points fall above the fitted line? How many fall below?

2. If a country had a 185-day school year, what percent correct would you predict? Do you think the test results would give exactly this percentage?

3. Why do we need a method for drawing a line? Why can't we just sketch one?

4. For a point that is above this line, describe how its actual percent correct compares to the percent described by this line.

5. To judge how much a country's actual percent differs from the value predicted by this line, we measure the vertical distance from the point to the fitted line. Which country is farthest above the line, and by how much?

6. Which country did the poorest in comparison to its prediction based on the length of their school years?

7. Name any other countries that you feel did relatively well or poorly in comparison to the prediction based on the length of their school years.

8. Find the point for the United States and describe its position.

9. Do you think the school year in the United States should be longer?

10. Do you think that lengthening the school year in a country would automatically increase student scores on this type of test? List several other factors that might be involved.

11. Suppose a country has a 250-day school year. Discuss why or why not it would make sense to predict its percent correct by extending and using the fitted straight line.

12. You might wonder why the fitted line has been constructed this way. Why have we used medians instead of means to form the X's? Why have we constructed three X's instead of two or four? Why have we constructed the slope of the line by using only the two end X's? After connecting the two end X's, why did we slide the ruler one-third of the way towards the middle X rather than some other fraction? Try to think of reasons for these choices or of alternate reasons for constructing a fitted line in a different way.

Application 29

Smoking and Heart Disease

The following table lists 21 countries with the cigarette consumption per adult per year and the number of deaths per 100,000 people per year from coronary heart disease (CHD).

Country	Cigarette Consumption per Adult per Year	CHD Mortality per 100,000 (Ages 35–64)
United States	3,900	257
Canada	3,350	212
Australia	3,220	238
New Zealand	3,220	212
United Kingdom	2,790	194
Switzerland	2,780	125
Ireland	2,770	187
Iceland	2,290	111
Finland	2,160	233
West Germany	1,890	150
Netherlands	1,810	125
Greece	1,800	41
Austria	1,770	182
Belgium	1,700	118
Mexico	1,680	32
Italy	1,510	114
Denmark	1,500	145
France	1,410	60
Sweden	1,270	127
Spain	1,200	44
Norway	1,090	136

Source: *American Journal of Public Health.*

1. In which country do adults smoke the largest number of cigarettes?

2. Which country has the highest death rate from coronary heart disease?

3. Which country has the lowest death rate from coronary heart disease?

4. If we want to predict CHD mortality from cigarette consumption, which variable should be placed on the horizontal axis of a scatter plot?

5. a) Make a scatter plot of the data.

   b) Draw two vertical lines so there are seven points in each strip.

   c) Place an X in each strip at the median of the cigarette consumption and the median of the CHD mortality.

d) Do the three X's lie close to a straight line?

e) Draw in the fitted line.

6. a) Which three countries lie the farthest vertical distance from the line?

b) How many units do they lie from the line?

c) Considering the cigarette consumption, are these countries relatively high or low in CHD mortality?

7. If you were told that the adults in a country smoke an average of 2,500 cigarettes a year, how many deaths from CHD would you expect?

8. If you were told that the adults in a country smoke an average of 1,300 cigarettes a year, how many deaths from CHD would you expect?

9. (For class discussion.) Consider how the cigarette consumption and CHD mortality data might have been gathered. What underlying information is needed to compute both rates? How do you think this information could have been obtained?

10. (For class discussion.) Sometimes strong association in a scatter plot is taken to mean that one of the variables *causes* the other one. Do you think that a high CHD death rate could cause cigarette consumption to be high? Could high cigarette consumption cause the CHD death rate to be high? Sometimes, though, there is not a causal relationship between the two variables. Instead, there is a hidden third variable. This variable could cause both of the variables to be high simultaneously. Do you think that this might be the situation for this example? Can you think of such a possible variable?

11. (For students who have studied algebra.) Choose two points on the fitted line and from them find the equation of the line. Express it in the form $y = mx + b$, where y is mortality from coronary heart disease per 100,000 people (aged 35–64) per year, and x is cigarette consumption per adult per year. Using this equation, how many additional deaths per 100,000 people tend to result from an increase of 200 in cigarette consumption? What number of cigarettes per year is associated with one additional death from CHD per 100,000 people per year?

SECTION VIII: LINES ON SCATTER PLOTS

Application 30

Animal Gestation and Longevity

The following table gives the average gestation (length of pregnancy) or incubation period (time from when an egg is laid until it hatches) in days and the average life span in years for 22 selected animals.

Animal	Average Gestation or Incubation Period (Days)	Average Life Span (Years)
Chicken	22	8
Duck	28	10
Groundhog	32	7
Rabbit	33	7
Kangaroo	36	5
Squirrel	44	9
Fox	57	9
Wolf	61	11
Cat	63	11
Dog	63	11
Lion	108	10
Pig	116	10
Goat	151	12
Sheep	151	12
Monkey	205	14
Bear	210	23
Hippopotamus	240	30
Deer	250	13
Human	278	73
Cow	280	11
Horse	336	23
Elephant	624	35

Source: New York Zoological Society.

The animals are listed by increasing order of average gestation period, so reading down the column of average life spans suggests a positive association between these variables. This application investigates additional aspects of the relationship between average gestation period and average life span.

1. Make a scatter plot with the average life span of these animals on the vertical axis and their average gestation or incubation period on the horizontal axis. Note that there are two data values of (63 days, 11 years), and two of (151 days, 12 years). Be sure that your scatter plot indicates that there are two observations at each of these points.

2. Does your scatter plot show positive association?

3. Fit a straight line to the scatter plot. Start by dividing the points into three groups with seven on each end and eight in the center.

4. One animal is farthest from the fitted line and is clearly an outlier in terms of these variables. Find its name and write a sentence describing how its position differs from the relationship among the other animals.

5. The elephant has the longest gestation period of these animals. Considering only the gestation variable, would you say that the elephant is an outlier? Now considering both variables and the relationship between average life span and average gestation period, would you say that the elephant is an outlier? Write a sentence explaining why or why not.

6. Apart from the animals in questions 4 and 5, name any other animals in this list that you feel have an average life span substantially larger or shorter than what is predicted from their gestation periods by your fitted straight line.

7. Notice that the column heading says, "Average Gestation or Incubation Period," although we have shortened this phrase to "gestation period" in most of the questions. Name the animals in the table that have an incubation rather than a gestation period. Do these animals seem to follow the same general relationship as the others, or do they fall substantially above or below the fitted line?

8. As the gestation period increases, do the differences between the average life spans and the predicted values tend to increase, decrease, or stay approximately the same size? Do these differences tend to become systematically positive or negative as gestation period increases?

9. (For students who have studied algebra.) Find the equation of the fitted line. Express it in the form $y = mx + b$; where x is the average gestation period (in days), y is the average life span (in years), b is the intercept, and m is the slope. According to this equation, if one animal has gestation period 50 days longer than a second animal, how much longer average life span would we expect the first animal to have than the second? If an animal has a gestation period of 300 days, what average life span does the equation predict?

Application 31

Science Achievement

We discussed the international assessment of science and mathematics achievement of 13-year-old students earlier in this section, beginning on page 116. Among the additional variables collected from each country participating in this study were the following: average minutes of science instruction each week; the percent of students who spend two hours or more on homework per day; and the percent of students who watch television five hours or more per day. The following table includes these variables along with the percent correct on the science test (which are the same numbers given earlier). In this application, we investigate questions concerning the relationship across countries between science achievement and each of these variables.

Area	Average Minutes of Science Instruction Each Week	Percent of Students Who Spend 2 Hours or More on Homework	Percent of Students Who Watch Television 5 Hours or More	Percent Correct For Science
Canada	156%	26%	15%	69%
France	174	55	4	69
Hungary	207	61	16	73
Ireland	159	66	9	63
Israel	181	49	20	70
Italy	138	78	7	70
Jordan	180	54	10	57
Scotland	179	15	23	68
Slovenia	283	27	5	70
South Korea	144	38	10	78
Soviet republics (Russia)	387	52	19	71
Spain	189	62	11	68
Switzerland	152	21	7	74
Taiwan	245	44	7	76
United States	233	31	22	67

Source: National Center of Education Statistics, *Learning Mathematics and Learning Science, 1992.*

1. How many minutes of science instruction do you receive each week? Do you typically spend two hours or more on homework per day? Do you typically watch television five hours or more per day?

2. (Class Exercise.) Combine the answers from question 1 for all the students in your class. How does your class compare with the values for the United States? Is there any reason why your class would not be typical?

For the following questions, the class should be divided into four groups. Each group should answer one of questions 3, 4, 5, and 6. The groups' results can be combined to answer question 7.

3. In this question, you will investigate the relationship between science percent correct and minutes of science instruction.

   a. Make a scatter plot with science percent correct on the vertical axis against average minutes of science instruction on the horizontal axis.

   b. Does the scatter plot suggest positive, negative, or no association?

   c. Use the procedure for fitting a straight line to put the three X's on your plot.

   d. Decide whether or not the three X's lie close to a straight line. If they do, draw the fitted line on your scatter plot. Write a sentence or two describing the relationship between science percent correct and minutes of science instruction each week.

4. Repeat question 3 using science percent correct and the percent of students who spend two hours or more on homework each day.

5. Repeat question 3 using science percent correct and the percent of students who watch television five hours or more each day.

6. Repeat question 3 to consider the relationship between the television variable (vertical axis) and the study variable (horizontal axis).

7. Write a story suitable for your school newspaper that summarizes these data in terms of the relationships between science achievement and the other variables. Include information from the average days of instruction per year that we studied earlier in this section. Be sure to mention how the United States compares to the other countries in terms of these variables and relationships.

Fitted Straight Lines — A More Complicated Example

When the scatter plot has more points on it than in the previous examples, we can still use the method that was described to fit a straight line. However, some parts of the construction and interpretation of the scatter plot can be more complicated, so we will now work a larger example.

The following scatter plot shows the weights and heights of 52 men in an office. Notice that in several places there is a "2" in the plot. This means that two men had the same height and weight.

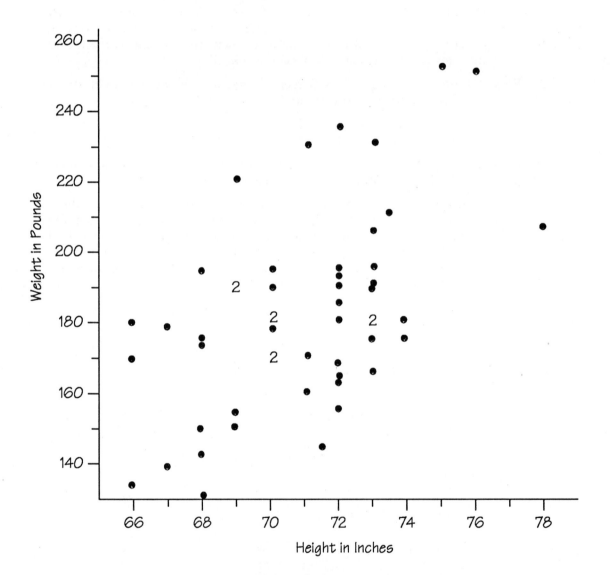

There are 52 points, so to construct the fitted line we would like to divide the points into three groups of as close to equal size as possible, say groups of 17, 18, and 17 points. This division is not possible because different men have the same height. For example, for the left group there are 16 men with heights 69" or less and 23 men with heights 70" or less. We cannot construct a group with exactly 17 men, so we choose the group with 16 by making the dividing line at 69.5". For the right group, counting in from the right side of the plot shows that 15 men have heights 73" or taller and 25 men have heights 72" or taller. Similarly, we choose the dividing point to be 72.5" so the right group has 15 points. This choice leaves 21 points in the middle. The dividing lines are shown in the following scatter plot.

Next we find the centers of the three groups using the median method. For the left group of 16 points, both the eighth and ninth largest heights are 68", so the median height is 68". For the weights, the eighth largest is 170 and the ninth is 175, so the median weight is 172.5 pounds. These medians give the left X on the scatter plot. For the right group of 15 points, the eighth height is 73" and the eighth weight is 190 pounds. These medians give the right X on the plot. Similarly, the center X is obtained from the 21 points in the center group as before.

The scatter plot with the three X's follows. It is important to stop now and see if the three X's fall reasonably close to a straight line. If they do not, we would not continue to fit the straight line.

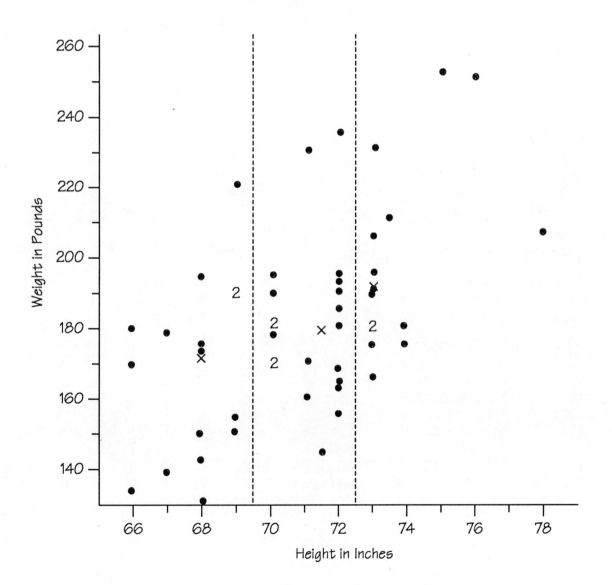

In this case the three X's are close to a straight line, so we continue. Draw the fitted line by first taking a straightedge and placing it along the two end X's. The middle X is below this line. We now slide the straightedge down one-third of the way towards the middle X and draw in the fitted line. This line is shown in the following scatter plot.

The fitted line does not go exactly through any of the three X's, but it goes close to each of them. From this straight line we can predict that a typical weight for a man 66" tall is 160 pounds, and a typical weight for a man 76" tall is 197 pounds. For a 10" increase in height there is a typical increase in weight of 37 pounds, so we could say that on the average for each one-inch increase in height there is a 3.7 pound increase in weight. It would be difficult to draw a conclusion like this without fitting a line to the scatter plot.

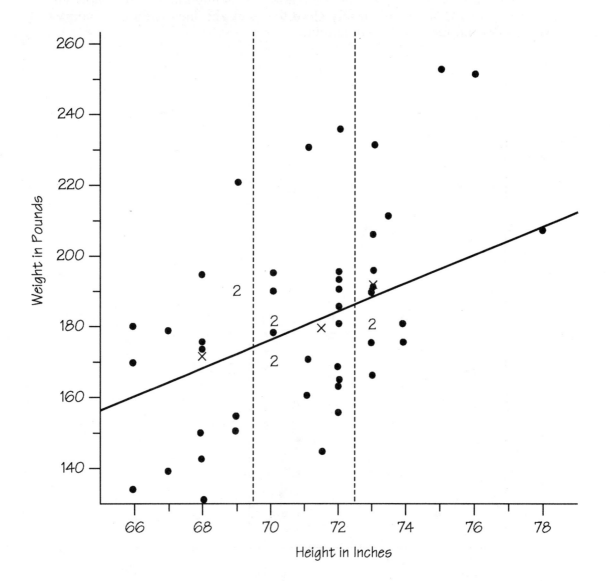

It is also useful to examine the spread of the points about the fitted line. A good way to do this is to add two additional lines that are parallel to the fitted line. We want these new lines to be an equal distance above and below the fitted line. We also want them drawn far enough from the fitted line so that most, but not all, of the points lie between the two new lines. This lets us notice and focus our attention more easily on outlying points or on other unusual features of the data around the edges.

This has been done in the following plot using lines giving weights that are 30 pounds more, and 30 pounds less, than the predicted weight for each height. The value 30 pounds was chosen by sliding a ruler parallel to the fitted line so that most, but not all, of the points would fall between these additional lines.

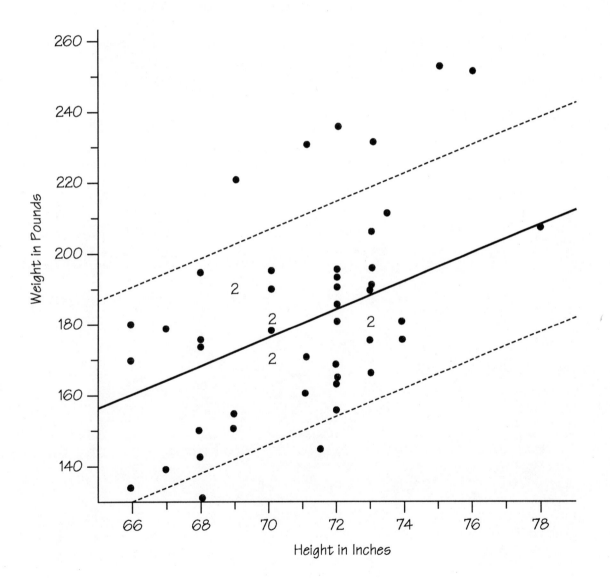

Discussion Questions

1. How many men fall above the top line? below the bottom line? How would you describe a man who falls above the top line?

2. What percentage of these 52 men would you say are unusually heavy for their height?

3. What percentage of these 52 men would you say are unusually light for their height?

4. Are there more men who are very heavy for their height, or are there more men who are very light for their height? Why do you think this is the case?

5. For those men whose weights are unusually heavy or unusually light for their heights, which group has the more extreme values of weight?

6. Find the man with height 78".

   a. How many men are heavier than he?

   b. Do you think he is overweight? Why or why not?

Application 32

The Beatles, Elvis, and The Supremes

The three artists with the most Number 1 records of all time are the Beatles with 20 Number 1 records, Elvis Presley with 17, and the Supremes with 12. (A Number 1 record is one that made the top position on the *Billboard* charts.) The following tables list all of the Number 1 records by these artists along with the year, the total number of weeks the record was Number 1, and the total number of weeks it was in the Top 40.

The Beatles	Year	Number of Weeks No. 1	Number of Weeks In Top 40
"I Want To Hold Your Hand"	1964	7	14
"She Loves You"	1964	2	14
"Can't Buy Me Love"	1964	5	9
"Love Me Do"	1964	1	11
"A Hard Day's Night"	1964	2	12
"I Feel Fine"	1964	3	11
"Eight Days A Week"	1965	2	9
"Ticket To Ride"	1965	1	9
"Help!"	1965	3	12
"Yesterday"	1965	4	9
"We Can Work It Out"	1965	3	11
"Paperback Writer"	1966	2	10
"Penny Lane"	1967	1	9
"All You Need Is Love"	1967	1	9
"Hello Goodbye"	1967	3	10
"Hey Jude"	1968	9	19
"Get Back"	1969	5	12
"Come Together"	1969	1	16
"Let It Be"	1970	2	13
"The Long and Winding Road"	1970	2	10

Elvis Presley	Year	Number of Weeks	
		No. 1	In Top 40
"Heartbreak Hotel"	1956	8	22
"I Want You, I Need You, I Love You"	1956	1	19
"Don't Be Cruel / Hound Dog" (2-sided hit)	1956	11	24
"Love Me Tender"	1956	5	19
"Too Much"	1957	3	14
"All Shook Up"	1957	9	22
"(Let Me Be Your) Teddy Bear"	1957	7	18
"Jailhouse Rock"	1957	7	19
"Don't"	1958	5	16
"Hard Headed Woman"	1958	2	14
"A Big Hunk O'Love"	1959	2	10
"Stuck On You"	1960	4	13
"It's Now or Never"	1960	5	16
"Are You Lonesome To-night?"	1960	6	14
"Surrender"	1961	2	11
"Good Luck Charm"	1962	2	11
"Suspicious Minds"	1969	1	13

The Supremes	Year	Number of Weeks	
		No. 1	In Top 40
"Where Did Our Love Go"	1964	2	13
"Baby Love"	1964	4	12
"Come See About Me"	1964	2	13
"Stop! In The Name Of Love"	1965	2	10
"Back In My Arms Again"	1965	1	10
"I Hear A Symphony"	1965	2	10
"You Can't Hurry Love"	1966	2	11
"You Keep Me Hangin' On"	1966	2	10
"Love Is Here And Now You're Gone"	1967	1	10
"The Happening"	1967	1	10
"Love Child"	1968	2	15
"Someday We'll Be Together"	1969	1	15

Source: *The Billboard Book of Top 40 Hits*, 1989.

There are many different ways to rank artists by their popularity. For example, it is easy to say that the Beatles had the most Number 1 records, and therefore they should be ranked at the top. Alternatively, we could compare the total number of hit records, or total sales, and these might give different rankings.

In this application, we investigate which of these artists' Number 1 records were most popular at the time they were hits. Are there any differences among these artists in this regard?

We can think of this question as assessing the "staying power" of these Number 1 hits. Did the Number 1 hits from any of these artists seem to be substantially more popular—have more "staying power"—than the Number 1 hits of the other two? Here we measure popularity using two compatible variables: the total number of weeks the record was Number 1 and the total number of weeks it appeared in the Top 40 charts.

1. Construct three box plots below the same scale to display the distributions of the number of weeks these hits were Number 1 for the Beatles, for Elvis, and for the Supremes.

2. Which artist or group had Number 1 hits that generally spent the most weeks in the top position? Is your decision obvious, or is it a close call?

3. Write a sentence or two describing the three box plots.

4. The box plot for the Supremes shows smaller numbers than those for Elvis and the Beatles. Is this because the Supremes had fewer Number 1 hits? Explain why or why not.

We next compare the Beatles and Elvis Presley using both variables: the number of weeks each hit was Number 1, and the number of weeks each appeared in the Top 40. To make the comparisons between the Beatles and Elvis easier, the scatter plots you will construct in questions 5 and 6 should be exactly the same size and use exactly the same scales. The plots can then be compared easily by placing them next to each other or on top of one another. But constructing the plots in this way requires some advance planning. Use a scale of 0 to 12 for weeks as Number 1, and use a scale of 0 to 25 for weeks in the Top 40. These choices include the largest and smallest values for both the Beatles and Elvis, so all the data points will fit inside the plots.

For the following questions, the class should be divided into two groups. Students in one group answer questions 5 and 8, and students in the other group answer questions 6 and 9. Students from both groups should combine their results and work together to answer questions 7, 10, and 11.

5. Construct a scatter plot of the number of weeks in the Top 40 against the number of weeks as Number 1 for the Beatles hits.

6. Construct a scatter plot of the number of weeks in the Top 40 against the number of weeks as Number 1 for the Elvis Presley hits.

7. Compare the two scatter plots from questions 5 and 6 by placing them next to or on top of one another. Write a sentence comparing the locations of the points in the two plots.

8. Adding a straight line to both scatter plots helps to compare them and to quantify the differences between the plots. For the Beatles scatter plot:

   a. Use the procedure for fitting a straight line to divide the points into three vertical strips and construct the X's marking the center of the points in each strip. (You will have to use reasonable judgment to divide the points into three vertical strips of as close to equal size as possible.)

b. Even though the scatter of the data points is not as linear in appearance as we might hope for, use the three X's to construct the fitted line and draw it on the scatter plot.

c. Suppose a Beatles hit record was Number 1 for a total of six weeks. About how many weeks would you expect it to be in the Top 40?

d. Did any Beatles hit appear in the Top 40 list for more than five weeks longer than the number of weeks that would be predicted for it? To answer this question using the plot and without doing arithmetic, hold a straight edge over the fitted line and slide the straight edge parallel and up five units on the vertical axis. Are there any data points remaining above the straight edge? For any such point, give the record's title.

9. Repeat questions 8a, 8b, 8c, and 8d for the Elvis Presley scatter plot.

10. Suppose the Beatles and Elvis each had hit records that spent the same number of weeks at Number 1. Which record would you expect to spend more weeks in The Top 40? Write a few sentences summarizing and quantifying the difference using the fitted lines from questions 8b and 9b.

11. (For class discussion.) An alternative way to use these data to arrive at the kinds of comparisons you made in question 7 would be to make only one scatter plot, but show the points for the Beatles and Elvis using different symbols; for example, B for the Beatles and E for Elvis. Do you think this would be harder or easier than what you did? Do you think it would show the differences more or less clearly? Do you think this approach would make it easier or harder to fit the lines in questions 8b and 9b?

Fitted Straight Lines — Clustering and Curvature

In the previous section, there were many scatter plots that could be appropriately fitted with straight lines. However, it isn't always appropriate to fit a straight line to a scatter plot. Sometimes the points do not lie near a single straight line. Two other possibilities are that the data could be *clustered* into two or more groups in the scatter plot or that the data might fall near a *curved* (not straight) line.

How can we tell if there is clustering or curvature, and what should we do about them? Look at the scatter plot as a whole, as you did in Section VII, to see if you observe clusters or a curved relationship. Sometimes clusters or curvature are more obvious after a straight line has been fitted. Always look at a plot again after fitting a line to see if something is apparent that wasn't before.

In some cases, a straight line fits well within one of the clusters but not to all the data. In that case, use this line for prediction or summary within the range of data corresponding to the cluster, but don't use a single line that is fitted to all the data. Sometimes you might fit two separate straight lines to different parts of the data. These lines can help you see that a single straight line does not fit well and that a curve might be better. Of course, you might decide instead that no straight or curved line fits well and none should be used for prediction or summary. This could be the best answer.

The following two applications have scatter plots containing clustering and curvature. For these plots, it is best not to interpret the data in terms of a single straight-line fit.

Application 33

Telephone Office Costs (Clustering)

The following scatter plot involves some engineering data. The horizontal axis gives the number of telephone lines that can be handled by each of 20 telephone switching offices. (A telephone switching office is the place where local telephone calls pass through and where one customer is connected to another.) The vertical axis gives an estimate of the total cost of constructing the office. The cost depends on more than just the number of telephone lines. Each point in the scatter plot represents one telephone switching office. The horizontal value is the number of telephone lines into the office and the vertical value is the total cost. We want to study the scatter plot to learn whether or not there is a close relationship between cost and capacity for these switching offices.

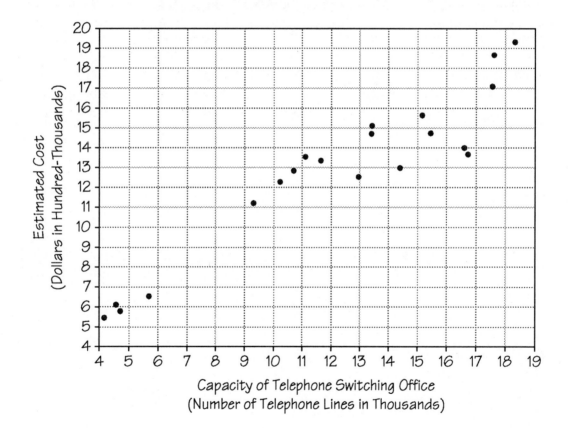

The first general impression is that there is a large gap in the data, giving two separate groups of switching offices. The bottom four offices are all separated by over 3,000 lines from the smallest of the other 16. You might think the topmost three points should also be treated as a separate cluster. Perhaps they should be, but the gap on the horizontal axis here is definitely smaller—only about 1,000 lines. Thus, as a first step, it seems sensible to treat the data as two clusters rather than one or three.

The data values for the 20 offices are listed in the following table. You will need to construct or trace a scatter plot such as the preceding one to answer the following questions.

Switching Office Capacity (Lines)	Estimated Cost	Switching Office Capacity (Lines)	Estimated Cost
4,200	$560,000	13,200	$1,470,000
4,600	610,000	13,300	1,510,000
4,700	580,000	14,400	1,300,000
5,700	660,000	15,200	1,580,000
9,300	1,120,000	15,500	1,480,000
10,200	1,230,000	16,700	1,400,000
10,700	1,270,000	16,800	1,370,000
11,100	1,360,000	17,600	1,710,000
11,600	1,340,000	17,700	1,870,000
13,000	1,250,000	18,400	1,930,000

1. For an office with 5,000 telephone lines, what cost would you estimate? Do not fit any straight line. Just scan the plot to get an estimate.

2. Fit a straight line to the cluster of 16 larger offices.

3. For offices of about 18,000 telephone lines, what cost does this line predict?

4. Extend the fitted line to the extreme left of the plot. What would it predict as the cost for an office of size 5,000?

5. How well does the line fit the four switching offices with small capacity? For what size offices does the fitted line give reasonable estimates of cost?

Tree Age and Diameter (Curvature)

The table below lists 27 chestnut oak trees planted on a poor site with their ages and diameters at chest height. We would like to determine how their size increases with age.

Age in Years	Diameter at Chest Height in Inches
4	0.8
5	0.8
8	1.0
8	2.0
8	3.0
10	2.0
10	3.5
12	4.9
13	3.5
14	2.5
16	4.5
18	4.6
20	5.5
22	5.8
23	4.7
25	6.5
28	6.0
29	4.5
30	6.0
30	7.0
33	8.0
34	6.5
35	7.0
38	5.0
38	7.0
40	7.5
42	7.5

Source: Chapman and Demeritt, *Elements of Forest Mensuration.*

1. Make a scatter plot of these data. We want to predict diameter given age. Which variable will you put on the horizontal axis?

2. Divide the points into three strips. Mark the three X's and draw in the fitted line.

3. Do the three X's lie very close to a single straight line?

4. In the left strip, how many points are

   a. above the line?

   b. below the line?

5. In the center strip, how many points are

   a. above the line?

   b. below the line?

6. In the right strip, how many points are

   a. above the line?

   b. below the line?

There are too many points above the line in the center strip and too many points below the line in both end strips. This means that a single straight line does not fit these data well. A curved line would summarize these data better. There are more complicated statistical methods for fitting a curve to data, but we will not investigate them. You could draw a free-hand curve through the middle of the data.

7. The fact that the points lie on a curved line tells us that trees do not grow at the same rate over their lifetimes. Does the diameter increase at a faster rate when the tree is young or old?

Application 35

The Challenger Space Shuttle

On January 28, 1986, the *Challenger* space shuttle was launched from the Kennedy Space Center in Florida. Shortly into the flight it exploded, killing all seven crew members. After the accident, President Reagan appointed a commission headed by former Secretary of State William Rogers to find the cause. The Rogers Commission report included the following information.

The night before the launch there was a three-hour teleconference among people from the Kennedy Space Center, NASA (National Aeronautics and Space Administration), and the company that manufactured the solid rocket motors. The discussion focused on the predicted 31°F temperature at launch time and the possible effect of such a low temperature on O-ring performance. The O-rings seal the joints between different sections of the solid rocket motors. In essence, each O-ring is a large rubber washer about 35 feet in diameter and 1/4 inch thick. After a shuttle is successfully launched, the rocket motors are jettisoned into the ocean and recovered. The O-rings can then be examined for possible damage that occurred during the launch. Thus, data were available from 23 previous space shuttle launches giving the temperature at launch time and the number of incidents of O-ring damage in that launch.

During the teleconference the night before the *Challenger* launch, a data set and associated scatter plot, shown below, played an important role in the discussion. Each plotted point represents one of the seven shuttle flights that experienced some O-ring damage; the horizontal axis shows the temperature at launch, and the vertical axis shows the number of O-rings that sustained damage in these flights.

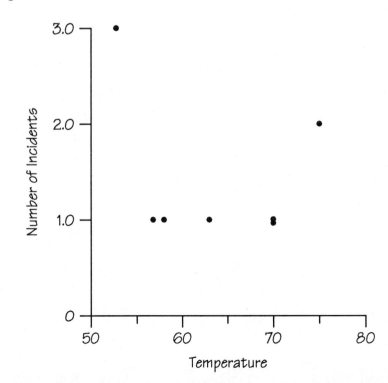

The teleconference participants debated whether these historical data implied a temperature effect on O-ring performance. Some participants recommended that the launch be postponed until the temperature rose above 53°F—the lowest previous launch temperature—because that flight had the largest number of damaged O-rings. Some participants also stated that separate physical evidence suggested a temperature effect on O-ring performance. On the other hand, the history showed that the second largest number of damaged O-rings occurred at the highest temperature. Ultimately, based on the U configuration of points in the scatter plot, it was concluded that there was no evidence from the historical data about a temperature effect. The official recommendation from the rocket manufacturer to NASA stated that the temperature data were not conclusive in predicting O-ring damage.

1. Do you think the preceding scatter plot suggests positive, negative, or no association between O-ring damage and temperature? How conclusive would you say these data are? Do you agree or not with the conclusion and recommendation of the teleconference participants?

The Rogers Commission concluded that the cause of the accident was the complete failure of an O-ring on a rocket motor, which lead to the explosion. This is the type of failure that was debated the night before in the teleconference, where the participants tried to decide whether the chance of extensive O-ring damage might be substantially increased by low temperature. The temperature at launch was 31°F.

The Rogers Commission also noted that a mistake had been made in the analysis of the historical data.

Before reading further, can you guess what this mistake was?

The mistake was that the flights with zero incidents of damaged O-rings were left off the plot because it was felt that these flights did not contribute any information about the temperature effect. The scatter plot including *all* the data is shown below.

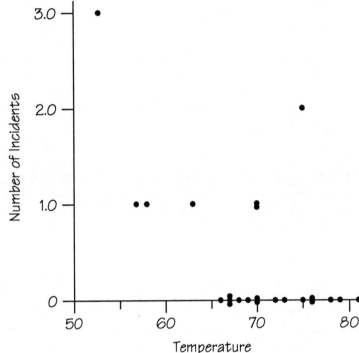

2. Do you think this scatter plot suggests positive, negative or no association between O-ring damage and temperature? How conclusive would you say these data are?

3. Based on these data, would you recommend launch at a temperature of 31°F?

4. Did you need to fit a line or use any complicated statistical technique to answer question 3?

The Rogers Commission concluded that "A careful analysis of the flight history of O-ring performance would have revealed the correlation of O-ring damage in low temperature."

The moral is that asking the right questions, understanding what information is needed to answer the questions, and analyzing the right data—all the data—are the most important parts of data analysis. Using the right data to deal with a problem is necessary. It is more valuable to be able to assess accurately whether the data you have are relevant to the important questions than it is to be able to perform or understand complicated statistical methods.

Source: This application is drawn from S. R. Dalal, E. B. Fowlkes, and B. Hoadley, "Risk analysis of the space shuttle: Pre-*Challenger* prediction of failure," *Journal of the American Statistical Association*, Vol. 84, pages 945–957.

Lines on Scatter Plots — Summary

The scatter plot is the basic method for learning about relationships between two variables. Sometimes interpretations are clear simply from studying the scatter plot. This section has dealt mostly with problems where the interpretation becomes clearer by adding a straight line to the plot.

The method of adding the $y = x$ line through the points (0, 0), (1, 1), (2, 2), and so forth and then observing on which side of this line most points lie can assist us in learning whether the variable on the horizontal axis or the variable on the vertical axis is generally larger. This method does not require fitting a line to the data.

In some examples, it is helpful to fit a straight line through the central part of the data. We have used a method based on medians. This method is not greatly affected by a few outlying points, but this method does require enough data points in each of the three sections so that each X is a reasonable measure for the center of the points in its section. If the data follow a straight-line relationship, the method described gives a line that fits the data closely. Moreover, looking at the data in terms of the three X's and the straight line can help us to recognize examples where the data do not fit a single straight line. These situations, such as clustering and curvature, need to be dealt with differently.

The critical feature about the $y = x$ line and the fitted straight line is not just the method of constructing them. As with all the other methods in this book, their purpose is to assist you in the interpretation and analysis of the data. These straight lines can help identify interesting and important data points, find and summarize relationships between the variables, and predict the variable on the vertical axis from the variable on the horizontal axis.

More important than any particular statistical method, however, is asking the right questions for the problem, understanding what information is needed to answer the questions, and analyzing the right data—*all* the data.

Suggestions for Student Projects

1. Take the scatter plots you made on your projects from Section VII and add straight lines when appropriate. Do the lines change any of your interpretations?

2. Many calculators have a button that fits a straight line to data on two variables. Often this button is labeled "least squares fit," "linear regression," or a shortened form of these expressions. The method to produce such a fitted line is not the same as the method explained in this book, which is called "median-median regression," "median fit line," or a similar expression with the word "median" in it.

   Consider one or several of the examples from this section in which you fitted a straight line through data using the method based on medians. Use a calculator to find the least squares fitted line. Plot this straight line on the scatter plot of the data along with the line based on medians. Do the two lines differ much? If they do, explain which line you think does a better job of representing these data and why.

   By working together with other students you can construct both types of fitted lines on several examples and compare the results. What overall conclusions can you reach concerning how these two methods for fitting a straight line differ? Do you prefer one method or the other in general? If so, explain why.

IX. TIME SERIES PLOTS

Some scatter plots have year (or some other time period) on the horizontal axis and one value for each year on the vertical axis. In such plots, connecting the points from one year to the next often helps show the general trend. For example, the following *plot over time,* or *time series plot,* shows how many 12-ounce soft drinks the average person in the United States drank each year from 1945 to 1991.

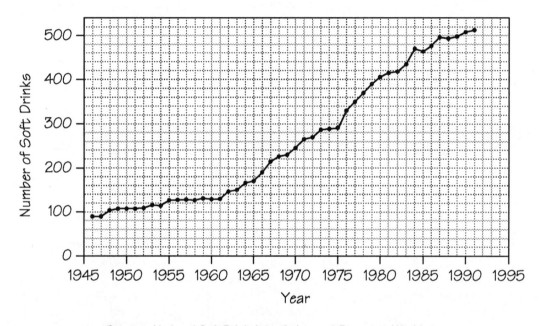

Source: National Soft Drink Association and *Beverage World.*

Discussion Questions

1. About how many soft drinks did the average person drink in 1950? in 1970?

2. About how many six-packs of soft drinks did the average person drink in 1980?

3. About how many soft drinks did the average person drink *per week* in 1950? in 1980?

4. When did the average person start drinking one or more soft drinks per day? About how many soft drinks per day did people average in 1990?

5. If the recent trend continues, about how many 12-ounce soft drinks will the average person drink in the year 2000?

6. In what year did soft drink consumption start to "take off"? Can you think of any reason for this?

7. Who is the "average person"?

8. Write a summary of the trend in soft drink consumption shown by the plot. (Our summary of this plot follows.)

149

In the United States from 1945 until 1961, soft drink consumption rose gradually from about 90 twelve-ounce servings per year per person to about 130 twelve-ounce servings. In 1962, soft drink consumption started to rise rapidly until it was about 400 twelve-ounce servings in 1980. In other words, in these 18 years, soft drink consumption per person more than tripled in the United States.

What happened in 1962? Some ideas are as follows:

- *Diet drinks might have been introduced.*

- *Soft drinks in aluminum cans might have become available.*

- *The economy might have improved so people started to spend more money on luxuries such as soft drinks.*

- *The post-war baby boom kids were reaching their teenage years.*

There were very big increases in the late 70's. In the 80's, consumption continued to increase, but at a somewhat lower rate. For example, in the five years from 1975 to 1980, per person consumption increased by 100 drinks from about 300 to 400; but it took the entire ten years from 1980 to 1990 to increase from 400 to 500. Especially in the late 80's and early 90's, the increase showed signs of leveling off. Perhaps the increasing popularity of fruit juice drinks, bottled natural water and flavored water, and iced tea drinks have cut into increases in the consumption of traditional soft drinks.

Application 36

Marriage Ages

The following table gives the median age at first marriage for men and women in the United States from 1900 to 1990 at ten-year time increments.

Median Age at First Marriage		
Year	Males	Females
1900	25.9	21.9
1910	25.1	21.6
1920	24.6	21.2
1930	24.3	21.3
1940	24.3	21.5
1950	22.8	20.3
1960	22.8	20.3
1970	23.2	20.8
1980	24.7	22.0
1990	26.1	23.9

Source: United States Bureau of the Census.

1. Of the women married in 1900 for the first time, what percentage of them were 21.9 years old or younger? From these data, can you determine the percentage of men married in 1900 for the first time who were age 30 or older? What can you say about this percentage?

2. Most people report their ages as integers or in years and months; for example, you say that you are "16 years old," or possibly "16 years and 4 months." What does an age of 21.9 represent in terms of years and months?

In order to see any patterns over time, the median ages at first marriage for males and females are displayed in the following time series plot with the points connected by straight lines.

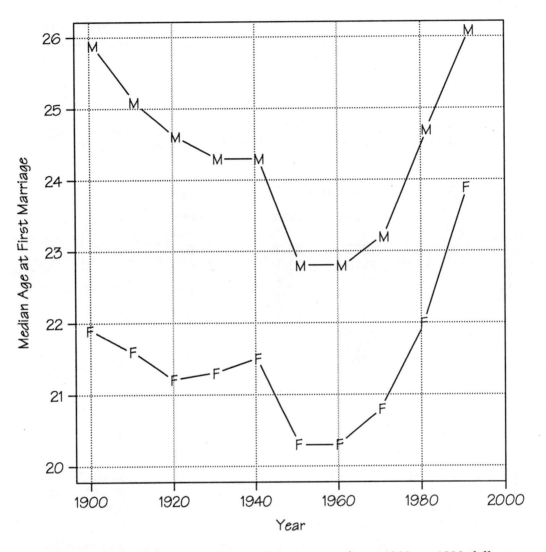

3. We see that both the male and female ages from 1900 to 1990 follow a similar overall pattern. Write a sentence or two describing this pattern.

4. During which decade did the largest decrease occur in median age at first marriage for men? for women? Give a possible explanation.

The median male age has been greater than the median female age at first marriage at all times from 1900 through 1990. The difference between the ages, however, appears to be smaller during recent years than during the early part of the century. This difference corresponds to the vertical distance in the plot between the two series of points. We can see some general characteristics of how the difference in median age changes over time by looking at the vertical distances. It is hard, however, to make precise comparisons of the distances because both the upper and lower ends vary from year to year. Thus, to investigate how the difference between the male and female median ages varies over time, it is worthwhile to make a separate, new time series plot of the differences.

5. Subtract the median female age at first marriage from the median male age for each year given in the data table, and construct a time series plot of these differences.

6. Describe any patterns you see in the time series plot of question 5.

7. What would you predict for the median age at first marriage in the year 2000 for males? for females? for the difference between the median ages? For which of these three quantities would you have the most confidence in your prediction?

8. Write an overall summary of the information displayed in both time series plots.

Application 37

Twenty-Seven Years of SATs

The following table gives the nationwide average SAT verbal and math scores for each year from 1967 through 1993.

	Average SAT Score	
Year	Verbal	Mathematics
1967	466	492
1968	466	492
1969	463	493
1970	460	488
1971	455	488
1972	453	484
1973	445	481
1974	444	480
1975	434	472
1976	431	472
1977	429	470
1978	429	468
1979	427	467
1980	424	466
1981	424	466
1982	426	467
1983	425	468
1984	426	471
1985	431	475
1986	431	475
1987	430	476
1988	428	476
1989	427	476
1990	424	476
1991	422	474
1992	423	476
1993	424	478

Source: The College Board.

From scanning the data table, it is evident that math scores are higher than verbal scores, and that the scores near the end of this time period are lower than the scores near the beginning. The following time series plot shows both verbal and math scores and allows us to explore these data in more detail.

154

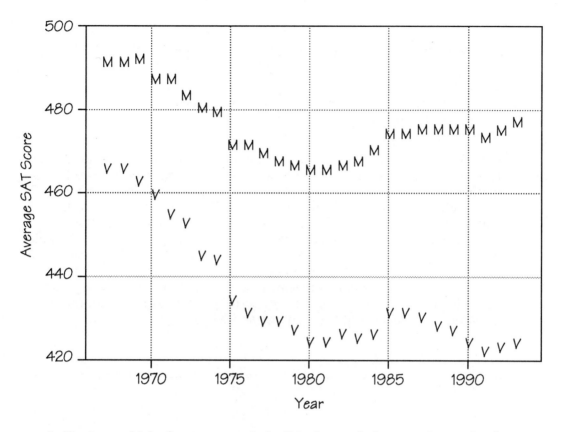

1. During which five-year period did the verbal score have the largest decrease?

2. Since the end of the time period of question 1, has the verbal score shown a net increase, shown a net decrease, or remained about the same?

3. During which five- or six-year period did the math score have the largest decrease?

4. Since the end of the time period of question 3, has the math score shown a net increase, shown a net decrease, or remained about the same?

5. Overall, which scores have decreased more, mathematics or verbal?

Question 5 raised the issue of whether math or verbal scores have decreased more over time. You will explore this question further in the following questions by constructing a new time series plot and analyzing it.

6. Calculate the average math score minus the average verbal score for each year. Construct a plot over time of these differences.

7. By about how much was the math average larger than the verbal average in the late 60's? in the early 90's?

8. Write a sentence summarizing the pattern over time of the difference between the scores.

9. Your plot from question 6 is a reasonable candidate for fitting a straight line. Use the median-based technique from Section VIII to fit a straight line to this plot. Explain why this straight line does or does not do a good job of summarizing these data.

10. (For students who have studied algebra.) Calculate the slope of the fitted line of question 9, and write a sentence describing what it represents in terms of the SAT scores.

11. Using the facts you discovered in the preceding questions, write a paragraph summarizing the behavior of the SAT average math and verbal scores over this 27-year time period.

12. (For class discussion.) Considering all your analyses of these data, do you feel that relatively greater attention needs to be paid to verbal or mathematics achievement? Do you think that nationwide average SAT scores give a good overall measure of student achievement in the United States over a long period of time? Concerning your analyses of these data, do you think it is more effective to obtain information from the data table or from the initial math and verbal time series plots? Explain the advantages and disadvantages of each. Suppose you want to communicate the information in these data to someone else, and you can use only one of the following: the data table, the time series plots, or your paragraph from question 11. Which would you choose and why?

Smoothing Plots Over Time

The following table lists the American League home run champions from 1921 to 1993.

Year	American League	HR	Year	American League	HR
1921	Babe Ruth, New York	59	1960	Mickey Mantle, New York	40
1922	Ken Williams, St. Louis	39	1961	Roger Maris, New York	61
1923	Babe Ruth, New York	41	1962	Harmon Killebrew, Minnesota	48
1924	Babe Ruth, New York	46	1963	Harmon Killebrew, Minnesota	45
1925	Bob Meusel, New York	33	1964	Harmon Killebrew, Minnesota	49
1926	Babe Ruth, New York	47	1965	Tony Conigliaro, Boston	32
1927	Babe Ruth, New York	60	1966	Frank Robinson, Baltimore	49
1928	Babe Ruth, New York	54	1967	Carl Yastrzemski, Boston	49
1929	Babe Ruth, New York	46		Harmon Killebrew, Minnesota	
1930	Babe Ruth, New York	49	1968	Frank Howard, Washington	44
1931	Babe Ruth, New York	46	1969	Harmon Killebrew, Minnesota	49
	Lou Gehrig, New York		1970	Frank Howard, Washington	44
1932	Jimmy Foxx, Philadelphia	58	1971	Bill Melton, Chicago	33
1933	Jimmy Foxx, Philadelphia	48	1972	Dick Allen, Chicago	37
1934	Lou Gehrig, New York	49	1973	Reggie Jackson, Oakland	32
1935	Jimmy Foxx, Philadelphia	36	1974	Dick Allen, Chicago	32
	Hank Greenberg, Detroit	58	1975	George Scott, Milwaukee	
1936	Lou Gehrig, New York	49		Reggie Jackson, Oakland	
1937	Joe DiMaggio, New York	46	1976	Graig Nettles, New York	32
1938	Hank Greenberg, Detroit	48	1977	Jim Rice, Boston	39
1939	Jimmy Foxx, Boston	35	1978	Jim Rice, Boston	46
1940	Hank Greenberg, Detroit	41	1979	Gorman Thomas, Milwaukee	45
1941	Ted Williams, Boston	37	1980	Reggie Jackson, New York	41
1942	Ted Williams, Boston	36		Ben Oglivie, Milwaukee	
1943	Rudy York, Detroit	34	1981	Bobby Grich, California	22
1944	Nick Etten, New York	22		Tony Armas, Oakland	
1945	Vern Stephens, St. Louis	24		Dwight Evans, Boston	
1946	Hank Greenberg, Detroit	44		Eddie Murray, Baltimore	
1947	Ted Williams, Boston	32	1982	Gorman Thomas, Milwaukee	39
1948	Joe DiMaggio, New York	39		Reggie Jackson, California	
1949	Ted Williams, Boston	43	1983	Jim Rice, Boston	39
1950	Al Rosen, Cleveland	37	1984	Tony Armas, Boston	43
1951	Gus Zernial, Chicago-Philadelphia	33	1985	Darrell Evans, Detroit	40
1952	Larry Doby, Cleveland	32	1986	Jesse Barfield, Toronto	40
1953	Al Rosen, Cleveland	43	1987	Mark McGwire, Oakland	49
1954	Larry Doby, Cleveland	32	1988	Jose Canseco, Oakland	42
1955	Mickey Mantle, New York	37	1989	Fred McGriff, Toronto	36
1956	Mickey Mantle, New York	52	1990	Cecil Fielder, Detroit	51
1957	Roy Sievers, Washington	42	1991	Jose Canseco, Oakland	44
1958	Mickey Mantle, New York	42		Cecil Fielder, Detroit	
1959	Rocky Colavito, Cleveland	42	1992	Juan Gonzalez, Texas	43
	Harmon Killebrew, Washington		1993	Juan Gonzalez, Texas	46

From this list it is difficult to see any general trends in the number of home runs through the years. To try to determine the general trends, we will make a scatter plot over time of the number of home runs hit by the champions and connect these points.

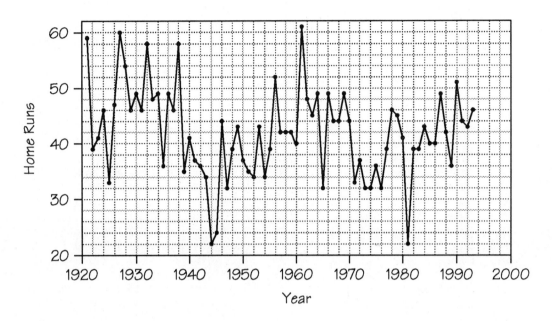

This scatter plot looks all jumbled up! It is difficult to see general trends because of the large fluctuations in the number of home runs hit from year to year. For example, 58 home runs were hit in 1938 compared to only 35 the next year. This variation gives the plot a sawtooth effect. The highs and lows, not the overall pattern, capture our attention. To remove the large fluctuations from the data and make it easier to detect any trends, we will use a method called *smoothing*.

To illustrate, the smoothed version of the first ten years of the home run champions' data follows.

Year	Home Runs	Smoothed Values
1921	59	59
1922	39	41
1923	41	41
1924	46	41
1925	33	46
1926	47	47
1927	60	54
1928	54	54
1929	46	49
1930	49	46
1931	46	

To find the smoothed value for 1924, for example, the 46 home runs for that year is compared to the number of home runs for the year before, 41, and the number of home runs for the following year, 33. The median of the three numbers, 41, is entered into the smoothed values column.

For the first and last years, just copy the original data into the smoothed values column.

The plot of the connected smoothed values follows. Notice what has happened to the large fluctuation between 1938 and 1939. Since this plot is smoother than the previous one, we can see general trends better, such as the drop in the number of home runs in the 1940's.

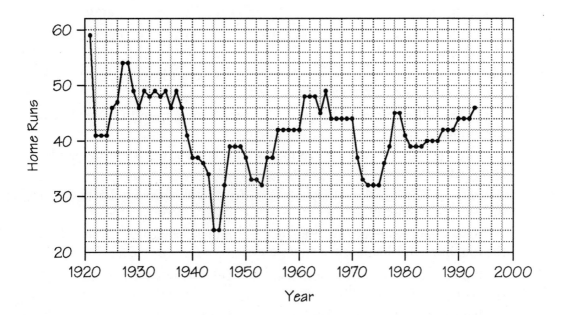

Discussion Questions

1. Complete the smoothed value column through 1940 for the next ten American League home run champions.

2. Study the smoothed plot of the American League home run champions.

   a. What happened around 1940 that could have affected the number of home runs hit?

   b. Did the increase in the number of games from 154 to 162 in 1961 have an effect on the number of home runs hit?

3. Study the following rule changes. Do any of them seem to have affected the number of home runs hit by the champions?

   1926—A ball hit over a fence that is less then 250 feet from home plate will not be counted as a home run.

   1931—A fair ball that bounces over a fence will be counted as a double instead of a home run.

   1959—New ballparks must have a minimum distance of 325 feet down the foul lines and 400 feet in center field.

   1969—The strike zone is decreased in size to include only the area from the armpit to the top of the knee.

   1969—The pitcher's mound is lowered, giving an advantage to the hitter.

   1971—All batters must wear helmets.

4. In 1981 there was a strike that shortened the season. Can this be seen in the original data? in the smoothed values?

5. Since they were not smoothed, the end points may appear to be out of place. The number of home runs hit in 1921 seems too high. Can you determine a better rule for deciding what to write in the smoothed values column for the end points?

6. Imagine a curve through the smoothed values. Try to predict the number of home runs hit in 2000.

7. In Section VIII, we learned how to fit a straight line to summarize a scatter plot. That method can be regarded as a way to smooth a scatter plot if we replace the original data by the corresponding points on the straight line. These points will certainly be smooth! A time series plot is just a special type of scatter plot. Explain, however, why it does not make sense to smooth the series of American League champion home runs by this method.

8. Some students feel that smoothing is not a legitimate method. For example, they do not like changing the original 33 home runs in 1925 to 46 home runs on the plot of smoothed values. Write a description of the trends that are visible in the smoothed plot that are not easily seen in the original plot. Try to convince a reluctant fellow student that smoothing is valuable. Then study the following answer. Did you mention features we omitted?

The original plot of the time series for home runs gives a very jagged appearance. There were values that were quite large for two years in the 1920's, two years in the 1930's, and also in 1961. Extremely low values occurred in the mid-1940's and in 1981. Using this plot, it is difficult to evaluate overall trends. However, the values in the 1940's and early 1950's seem lower than the values in the late 1920's and 1930's.

We get a stronger impression of trends from the smoothed plot of the home run data. In particular, for the years from 1927 to 1935, the values are generally higher than at any other time before or since. The only period that was nearly comparable was in the early 1960's. The original data show that the champions causing the earlier values to be large were Babe Ruth, Jimmy Foxx, and Lou Gehrig. In the 1960's, it was Roger Maris and Harmon Killebrew. These players clearly were outstanding home run hitters!

There was a steady decline in home runs from the late 1930's to a low period in the middle 1940's. There were also low periods in the early 1950's and in the early 1970's. It is interesting that these lows coincide roughly with World War II, the Korean War, and the Viet Nam War. These wars might be possible causes for the declines, although we have not proved this simply through observing this association. Since 1980, the values have been increasing steadily, although they have not reached the sustained high levels of the early 1930's and early 1960's. The smoothed series has removed some of the individual highs (such as Maris' 61 in 1961) and lows (such as the 22 in the strike-shortened 1981 season). Therefore, the longer trends stand out more clearly.

9. (Optional.) Consider the time series plots analyzed previously in Section IX for Applications 36, 37, and soda consumption. Would smoothing any of them be worthwhile to help identify trends in the data, or are the trends already clear enough in the original time series plot without smoothing? In general, if trends in the original series are clear and there is not a lot of short-term variability, then smoothing is not needed. On the other hand, sometimes smoothing helps a lot.

Airline Safety

The following table gives the number of fatal accidents per 100,000 aircraft departures for U.S. airlines for the 15 years from 1977 through 1991. This measure of airline safety can be interpreted as follows: If a commercial airplane trip has an accident (including sabotage) in which there is one fatality or more, then this event counts as one fatal accident in the numerator of the rate regardless of the total number of fatalities. The denominator measures the total number of airline flight segments. That is, in each segment an aircraft has a takeoff (departure), flight, and landing; this counts as one in the denominator.

Year	Fatal Accidents per 100,000 Departures	Smoothed Values
1977	0.061	
1978	0.100	
1979	0.074	
1980	0.000	
1981	0.077	
1982	0.060	
1983	0.079	
1984	0.018	
1985	0.069	
1986	0.016	
1987	0.061	
1988	0.045	
1989	0.166	
1990	0.087	
1991	0.059	

Source: U.S. National Transportation Safety Board.

1. Suppose there were 5 fatal accidents in a year and 5,800,000 aircraft departures. Calculate the fatal accident rate per 100,000 departures.

2. Suppose a frequent flyer takes one round trip each week that includes four departures (so there is an intermediate stop or transfer each way), and the traveler does this 50 weeks each year. How long will it take to reach a total of 100,000 departures?

3. Suppose a frequent flyer takes one round trip each week that includes four departures, and the traveler does this 50 weeks each year. Suppose the traveler continues this schedule for 50 years, and the fatal accident rate per 100,000 departures remains constant at 0.07 over this time period. What is the expected number of fatal accidents over all these flights?

4. Assuming the 1991 fatal accident rate, we can expect one fatal accident every how many flights?

5. The rate given here—fatal accidents per 100,000 departures—is not the only reasonable way to measure airline safety. Give an alternative measure of airline safety.

The time series plot for these data is given as follows. This plot is a good candidate for smoothing because of the sawtooth effect. This sawtooth appearance indicates that some points might be unusually large or small, and that overall patterns or trends might be seen more easily in the smoothed series.

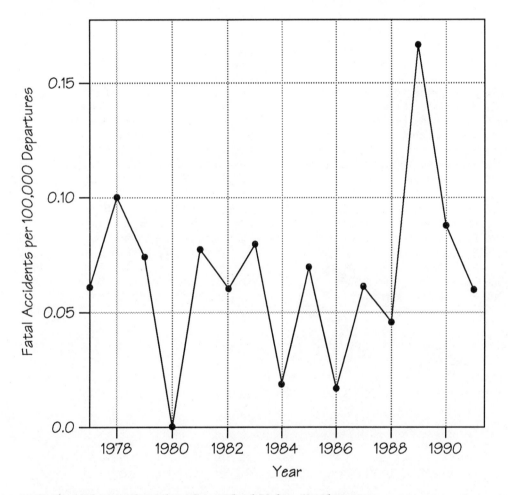

6. Copy and complete the "Smoothed Values" column.

7. Make a time series plot of the smoothed values.

8. Name any year(s) with an accident rate that differs from the trend by a large amount.

9. Does airline safety seem to be improving, getting worse, or staying about the same? Summarize the general trend in U.S. airline safety over these years.

Application 39

Olympic High Jump

The following table shows the winning heights for the high jump competitions in the 1928—1992 Olympics. The heights are given in feet and hundredths of a foot.

Year	Women Winner, Country	Height (feet)	Men Winner, Country	Height (feet)	Ratio
1928	Ethel Catherwood, Canada	5.21	Robert King, United States	6.38	0.817
1932	Jean Shiley, United States	5.44	Duncan McNaughton, Canada	6.46	0.842
1936	Ibolya Csak, Hungary	5.25	Cornelius Johnson, United States	6.67	0.787
1948	Alice Coachman, United States	5.50	John Winter, Australia	6.50	0.846
1952	Esther Brand, South Africa	5.48	Walter Davis, United States	6.71	0.817
1956	Mildred McDaniel, United States	5.77	Charles Dumas, United States	6.96	0.829
1960	Iolanda Balas, Romania	6.06	Robert Shavlakadze, USSR	7.08	0.856
1964	Iolanda Balas, Romania	6.23	Valery Brumel, USSR	7.15	0.871
1968	Miloslava Rezkova, Czechoslovakia	5.96	Dick Fosbury, United States	7.35	0.811
1972	Ulrike Meyfarth, West Germany	6.29	Yuri Tarmak, USSR	7.31	0.860
1976	Rosemarie Ackermann, East Germany	6.33	Jacek Wszola, Poland	7.38	
1980	Sara Simeoni, Italy	6.46	Gerd Wessig, East Germany	7.73	
1984	Ulrike Meyfarth, West Germany	6.63	Dietmar Moegenburg, West Germany	7.71	
1988	Louise Ritter, United States	6.67	Gennadiy Avdeyenko, USSR	7.81	
1992	Heike Henkel, Germany	6.63	Javier Sotomayor, Cuba	7.67	

Quickly scanning this table shows that the winning heights for both woman and men have generally increased over the years, and that the men's heights are greater than the women's heights. In this Application, we explore questions concerning comparisons of the women's heights to the men's heights.

1. What was the first year in which the women's winning height was greater than the men's 1948 winning height?

2. Suppose a winning height is 6 feet 5 inches. How would this value be represented in the table? Express 7.81 feet in terms of feet and inches.

3. Find the two years when the Olympics were not held. Why were the Olympics not held in these years?

4. Why are the countries for the women's winners in 1972, 1976, and 1984 given as "West Germany" and "East Germany," while the country for the 1992 winning woman is listed simply as "Germany"?

5. To compare the women's and men's results, we will construct the ratio of the women's winning height to the men's winning height for each year, and then analyze these values. The first ten ratios are filled in the previous table. Calculate the ratio of the women's winning height to the men's winning height for each of the remaining years.

6. Construct a plot over time with year on the horizontal axis and ratio of women's winning height to men's winning height on the vertical axis. Do not connect the points.

One way to obtain the smoothed plot of the time series of the ratios is to compute a new column of smoothed values from the ratios, and then construct a plot over time of the smoothed values. Alternatively, you can bypass the step of explicitly calculating the smoothed values as follows: Start with a time series plot of the ratios without adjacent points connected by straight lines. Consider the left end (beginning time point) of these data. The smoothed value for the first time is simply the corresponding observed value, so mark an X on top of this data point. It helps to use a different color for the new points. Next consider the second time; the smoothed value is the median of the data values for the first, second, and third times. The median must equal one of these three data values, and it is quick and easy to decide which one. Mark an X at the appropriate value on the vertical axis for the second time. Continue moving across the plot, at each stage finding the median of the data values for three adjacent times. You can use two straightedges to cover up all the points to the left and right of the three being considered, and then slide the two straightedges across the page. Finally, after you have an X marked for each time, connect the X's with straight lines. This is the smoothed time series.

7. Using either method described in the preceding paragraph, construct a plot over time of the smoothed ratios of women's to men's winning heights.

8. Write a paragraph summarizing the trends shown in the smoothed time series plot from question 7. Include in the paragraph your prediction of the ratio of women's to men's winning heights for the Olympics in the year 2000. Also include upper and lower limits that you are fairly certain will include this ratio for the Olympics in the year 2000.

9. (For class discussion.) We can also consider smoothing a time series plot by using the method given in Section VIII to fit a straight line to the plot. On the time series plot of the ratios from question 6, use the method of Section VIII to fit a straight line to these data. Does a straight line fit these data very well? What prediction does this line give for the ratio of the winning times for the Olympics in the year 2000? Overall, for this time series plot, does the smoothing method using the median of three adjacent points or the straight line seem to do a better job of representing the trends in these data? Explain your reasons.

Application 40

Carbon Dioxide, A Greenhouse Gas

Accurate data over long time periods are necessary for analyzing global environmental issues, in particular possible climatic changes caused by the greenhouse effect. The greenhouse effect occurs when the earth's atmosphere traps energy from the sun. Gases such as carbon dioxide (CO_2), water vapor, and methane allow incoming sunlight to pass through, but these gases absorb heat radiated back from the earth's surface. If the amount of these gases in the atmosphere increases sufficiently over time, then the earth will tend to heat up, as a greenhouse does.

Carbon dioxide is produced from burning fossil fuels (gasoline, oil, coal), from plants decaying, and by animals breathing. Surprisingly, long-ago levels of atmospheric carbon dioxide can be estimated by measuring air trapped in ice cores at the North and South Poles. Modern, precise atmospheric carbon dioxide measurements began in 1958 as part of the International Geophysical Year.

Measurements taken since 1958 at Mauna Loa, Hawaii, constitute the longest continuous record of atmospheric carbon dioxide concentrations available. This site is a barren lava field near an active volcano and is considered excellent for measuring undisturbed air, since there is little influence from vegetation or human activities. Researchers consider this to be the single most valuable carbon dioxide time series. The following plot shows these annual concentrations, measured in parts per million by volume of dry air (ppmv).

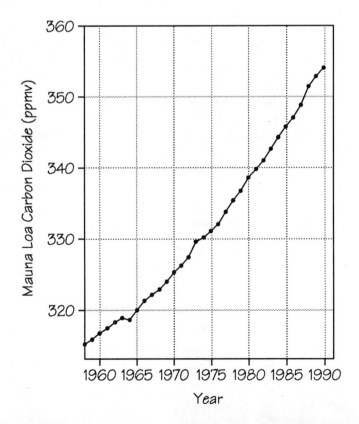

It is clear that atmospheric carbon dioxide at Mauna Loa has increased steadily over these 33 years. In fact, each value is larger than the previous year's (except for one year).

1. Place a straightedge next to the data points in the time series plot. Does a straight line adequately summarize these data?

2. Consider only the values from 1960 through 1970. Does a straight line do a better job of summarizing these points?

3. Use the plot to determine the concentrations in 1960 and 1970. By what percentage did the concentrations increase over this ten-year period?

4. Consider only the values from 1980 through 1990. Does a straight line summarize these data reasonably well? By what percentage did the concentrations increase over this ten-year period? Is the concentration increasing faster near the beginning or near the end of the 1958–1990 time period?

5. For a time series such as this one that is steadily increasing, would the median-based method of smoothing presented in this Section give any different impression of the trends than does the original data series itself? Explain why or why not.

Since 1958, shorter, carefully recorded time series of atmospheric carbon dioxide have been taken at about 50 sites around the world. We will compare three sites in North America to the readings at Mauna Loa, Hawaii. The questions we wish to explore concern to what extent the measurements at other sites are similar to, or different from, the Mauna Loa values.

The three sites are the following: Niwot Ridge, Colorado—an alpine mountain location that is about the same elevation as Mauna Loa—with measurements from 1968 through 1990; Key Biscayne, Florida—a coastal island seashore (near Miami)—with measurements from 1973 through 1990; and Sable Island, Nova Scotia, Canada—also an island seashore—with measurements from 1975 through 1990.

The following time series plot shows all four series on one plot. The original Mauna Loa values are plotted with solid dots and not connected. The Florida values are plotted using *F*, the Nova Scotia values using *N*, and the Colorado values using *C*. The points for each of these three series are connected when possible.

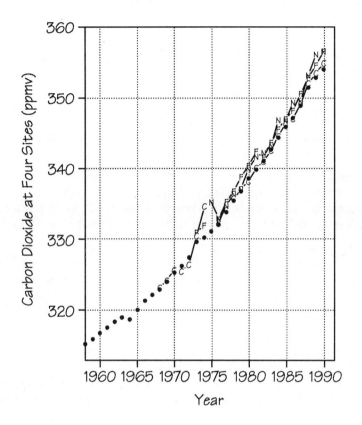

6. For certain years, it is difficult or impossible to distinguish the different plotting symbols because they are on top of each other. In this situation, what can we conclude about these data values?

7. Overall, can you distinguish any of the three series (*C, F,* and *N*) as clearly different from the Mauna Loa series? If so, explain how they differ.

The preceding time series plot offers convincing evidence that, overall, these four time series of atmospheric carbon dioxide are quite similar to each other. They may not be exactly the same, but they certainly seem to increase in similar ways over these years. There can be no doubt that yearly measurements of atmospheric carbon dioxide at these four widely scattered locations are closely related. The increase is clearly a global phenomenon (actually, from just these sites, it is a North American and mid-Pacific ocean phenomenon) and not an isolated regional phenomenon.

The preceding plot, however, does not enable us to determine whether or not there are any small yet systematic differences between atmospheric carbon dioxide at each of the three new sites and Hawaii. To investigate this question in detail, we need to perform additional calculations and construct new time series plots. We will calculate the difference between each new series and the Hawaii series (for their common years), plot this difference as a time series, smooth it, and interpret and compare the results. The following table contains the data.

Carbon Dioxide Concentrations
In the Atmosphere (Parts per Million by Volume)

Year	Mauna Loa, Hawaii	Niwot Ridge, Colorado	Key Biscayne, Florida	Sable Island, Nova Scotia, Canada
1958	315.2			
1959	315.8			
1960	316.8			
1961	317.5			
1962	318.3			
1963	318.8			
1964	318.6			
1965	319.9			
1966	321.2			
1967	322.0			
1968	322.8	323.1		
1969	323.9	324.1		
1970	325.3	325.6		
1971	326.2	325.4		
1972	327.3	326.3		
1973	329.5	330.3	330.8	
1974	330.1	334.5	331.8	
1975	331.0			335.1
1976	332.0	332.1	332.7	332.9
1977	333.7	334.8	335.2	334.6
1978	335.3	335.7	336.7	336.3
1979	336.7	337.0	338.7	336.9
1980	338.5	338.1	340.3	339.9
1981	339.8	340.0	342.3	341.6
1982	341.0	340.9	341.5	342.1
1983	342.6	342.4	343.5	343.2
1984	344.3	344.4	345.3	346.7
1985	345.7	346.1	346.8	346.6
1986	347.0	346.8	348.0	349.2
1987	348.8	349.0	350.4	349.3
1988	351.4	351.9	352.7	353.0
1989	352.8	353.3	354.4	355.9
1990	354.0	354.7	356.3	356.3

Source: U.S. Department of Energy, Oak Ridge National Laboratory Environmental Sciences Division, *Trends '91*. Annual values are used when reported. When no annual values are given but values for some months are reported, we use the median of all monthly values available in that year. Blanks indicate sites and years with no data.

For question 8, the class should be divided into three groups. Each group will construct and analyze a time series plot comparing one of the new sites to the Hawaii site. The groups can work together to compare the three plots in question 9. As with the scatter plot comparisons in Application 32, it is easier to compare the plots if they are all the same size and have the same horizontal and vertical scales, so the plots can be placed on top of one another. Make each horizontal scale extend from 1965 through 1990, and each vertical scale extend from −1.0 to 4.5.

8. For each of the Florida, Colorado, and Nova Scotia sites:

   a. Use the data table to subtract the Hawaii atmospheric carbonic dioxide reading from the reading for the new site; do this for each year having measurements for both sites.

   b. Construct a plot over time of these differences. Do not connect the points.

   c. Use the method based on medians to smooth this series. Use a different plotting character for the smoothed values than you used in question 8a, and connect the smoothed values.

   d. Summarize how atmospheric carbon dioxide at this site compares to that in Hawaii. Include information about any trend, as well as variability, in the differences.

9. Using the time series plots from question 8 for all three sites, compare the three sites in terms of the difference between each site and Mauna Loa. Include your assessment of which differences are the most consistently different from zero across these years.

10. Considering all the analyses in this application, write a paragraph summarizing the most important results about atmospheric carbon dioxide changes and relationships that have emerged.

11. (Extension.) The three plots of smoothed differences from question 8c exhibit some abrupt changes and to some extent a sawtooth appearance, although not as much as do the original series of differences. It might be helpful to smooth these data further in order to better display any underlying trends. A variation of the procedure for smoothing that will typically give a smoother appearance is to replace each value with the median of that value and the *two* values on either side. That is, we smooth by taking medians of five values rather than medians of three. Use this method to smooth the time series of differences for each of the three sites and connect the points. Do these series of smoothed values appear, in fact, to be smoother than were the earlier smooths from medians of three? Do the smooths from medians of five suggest trends more clearly—or do they suggest different trends—than the earlier smoothed series from medians of three?

Time Series Plots — Summary

A time series plot, also called a plot over time, is a scatter plot in which the horizontal axis represents time and there is one value plotted on the vertical axis for each time. Typically the time points are equally spaced, for example one day, or one year, or ten years. It is often helpful to connect the points in order to see the trend. Look for places where the general trend seems to change, and try to find possible explanations. If there is more than one time series on a plot, compare them to determine similarities and differences. Sometimes it helps to make a new plot of the differences or ratios between two time series.

By far the majority of all time series do not follow a straight line trend over a long period of time, so fitting a straight line to a time series plot using the method of Section VIII is generally not useful. However, time series plots can be smoothed by a technique based on taking medians of three adjacent data values. These medians can be interpreted as smoothed values, and these smoothed values can remove much of the sawtooth effect often seen in time series data. As a result, a clearer picture of where values are increasing and decreasing emerges.

Many students feel uncomfortable with smoothing. Try to think of it in the same way you think about computing, say, a mean. When you average your test scores in math, the original scores disappear and you are left with one number that summarizes how well you did overall. It is a similar idea with smoothing. Some of the original data disappear and you are left with a summary of overall trends.

Suggestions for Student Projects

1. Collect some time series data that interest you and analyze these data according to the methods of this section. Your topic might be one of the following:

   - the number of student absences in your class or school for each day of the last few months

   - daily sales in the school cafeteria during the last few months

   - the daily temperature maximums, minimums, or ranges as reported in the local newspaper

   - sports records for your school

2. Consider the alternative smoothing procedure described in Application 40, question 11. To use this procedure, replace each value with the median of that value and the *two* values on either side. For example, in the American League home run data, the smoothed value for 1924 would be 41, which is the median of 39, 41, 46, 33, and 47. These are the numbers of home runs hit in 1922, 1923, 1924, 1925, and 1926. Use this method of "smoothing by medians of five values" on other data sets in this section, and compare the results to those from smoothing using medians of three values. Discuss the advantages and disadvantages of the two methods.

171

X. REVIEW OF ALL TECHNIQUES

It might be helpful to reread the review of one variable techniques in Section VI before reading this section.

Two Variable Techniques

Suppose that we have measured the cumulative grade point average and the SAT score for each senior in a school. We want to learn how grade point averages and SAT scores are related. This is called a *two variable* situation since we have two values—grade average and test score—for each person.

The basic display for this situation is the scatter plot (Section VII). A scatter plot helps you determine if there is positive, negative, or no association between the variables. Of course, you must be careful about reaching conclusions from small data sets. And even with large amounts of data, the fact that two variables are associated does not imply that one variable causes the other. A scatter plot also helps you determine whether or not the data separate into several clusters of points and whether or not there are any outlying points that do not follow the general pattern. If you notice one of these features, try to find possible reasons for it as part of your interpretation.

After you construct and study a scatter plot, the relationship between the variables may be clear. If so, there is no need to supplement the scatter plot. However, important yet subtle interpretations, concerning both general relationships and specific data points, can often be brought out by adding an appropriate straight line to the scatter plot (Section VIII).

Often in scatter plots, one of the two variables is time. In these situations we have a plot over time, or time series plot (Section IX). For plots over time, smoothing can help to show long-run underlying trends, as well as departures of specific points from these trends.

The following applications will help you to see the relative advantages and disadvantages of the statistical methods described in Sections I–IX. No new techniques are given. These applications will take more time and thought than previous ones. There are fewer questions directing you through the analysis, and you will have to decide which plots work best.

There are no right or wrong answers to many of the questions. Your teacher will expect you to make appropriate plots and to write thoughtful and complete comments about the characteristics of the data shown in the plots.

Application 41

High School Sports Injuries

Which high school sports have the highest injury rates? A 13-year study of nearly 60,000 high school athletes in 18 sports was performed in the Seattle area to answer this and related questions. Some of the results are given in the table below.

Sport	Total Athletes	Number of Injuries per 100 Athletes	Percentage of Different Athletes Injured
Girls' Cross-Country	1,299	61.4	33.1
Football	8,560	58.8	36.7
Wrestling	3,624	49.7	32.1
Girls' Soccer	3,186	43.7	31.6
Girls' Gymnastics	1,082	38.9	26.2
Boys' Cross-Country	2,481	38.7	24.6
Boys' Soccer	3,848	36.4	25.2
Girls' Basketball	3,634	34.5	24.2
Boys' Basketball	3,874	29.2	22.9
Girls' Track	3,543	24.8	18.0
Volleyball	3,444	19.9	16.1
Softball	2,957	18.3	14.8
Boys' Track	4,425	17.3	13.6
Baseball	3,397	17.1	14.4
Fastpitch	134	11.9	11.9
Co-ed Swimming	4,004	8.3	6.4
Co-ed Tennis	4,096	7.0	5.8
Co-ed Golf	2,170	1.4	1.3

Source: *New York Times*, December 4, 1993.

1. Scan the table. Which sport is the most dangerous if we rank the sports by the total number of injuries per 100 athletes? Which is the safest? Which sport is the most dangerous if we rank the sports by the percentage of different athletes who are injured? Which is the safest according to this measure?

2. What is another important type of injury information not given in this table that would be useful for determining the safety of these sports?

The preceding table presents two variables measuring injuries: the number of injuries per 100 athletes, and the percentage of different athletes who are injured. Another related quantity of interest is the mean number of injuries per athlete for those athletes who are injured at all. This measure might be interesting because, in some sports, athletes who are injured might tend to be re-injured a large number of times, while other sports might tend to have fewer re-injuries among those athletes initially injured.

The mean number of injuries per injured athlete can be calculated from this table. For example, consider girls' basketball. Of 100 girls' basketball players, the table says we can expect a total of 34.5 injuries. The table also says that we can expect 24.2 of these 100 girls to receive an injury. The 34.5 injuries must be spread among these 24.2 girls, implying that the mean number of injuries per athlete for those who are injured at all is $34.5 \div 24.2 = 1.43$. That is, we can expect an average of about 1.4 injuries for a girls' basketball player who receives an injury.

3. For each of these sports, calculate the mean number of injuries per athlete for those athletes who receive any injury. Could this number ever be less than 1.00? Explain why or why not.

4. From the three available variables (two from the table and one from question 3), choose one that you think is the most reasonable overall measure of injuries. Construct a one variable plot displaying these values, making sure that any noteworthy values are labeled.

5. The variables "percentage of different athletes injured" and "mean number of injuries per athlete who is injured" measure logically separate aspects of injury, since the first variable concerns the proportion of athletes who receive any injury while the second concerns the number of injuries among those who are injured. To see if these variables are associated, construct a scatter plot with "percentage of different athletes injured" on the horizontal axis and "mean number of injuries per athlete who is injured" on the vertical axis. Make sure you label any noteworthy points.

6. Using the information from the previous questions and from any other plots or calculations that you think would be helpful, write a paragraph or two summarizing the results concerning injuries in high school sports.

Application 42

Time Use by Women

One way to study the lives of typical women in different countries is to measure what women do in the course of a week. Several countries have performed such time-use studies to gather information about their citizens. The United Nations collected the results and made adjustments to the data to account for different study procedures and definitions across the countries.

The following table summarizes the results of all 13 studies of women that were reported between 1975 and 1990. The "Economic Activity" column refers to time spent in income-earning activities, going to school, and doing unpaid work in family businesses. The "Unpaid Housework" column includes child care, cooking, shopping, laundry, and other unpaid housework. The "Personal Care and Free Time" column includes sleeping, eating, socializing, reading, watching television, and other similar activities. The units for each column are hours per week.

Country	Year of Study	Economic Activity	Unpaid Housework	Personal Care and Free Time
Bulgaria	1988	37.7	33.7	97
Australia	1987	16.9	33.0	118
Canada	1986	17.5	28.9	121
United States	1986	24.5	31.9	112
USSR	1986	38.5	30.1	99
Poland	1984	24.9	34.9	108
United Kingdom	1984	14.1	30.0	124
Venezuela	1983	15.5	32.2	120
Norway	1981	17.1	29.8	121
Netherlands	1980	7.1	33.4	130
Finland	1979	21.8	25.6	122
Guatemala	1977	29.4	49.7	89
Hungary	1976	26.7	33.3	108

Source: United Nations, *The World's Women 1970–1990.*

Here are some questions to investigate: Is the time women in these countries spent in economic activities closely associated either with time spent on unpaid household work or with free time? Is it possible to accurately predict either of the later two variables from time spent on economic activity? If so, what is the prediction and how can it be interpreted? Are there any countries that seem to be outliers from the relationships? How does the United States compare to the other countries in terms of how women use their time?

1. Your assignment is to construct the plots and perform the calculations to address the preceding questions. Write a paragraph or two describing your results.

2. (Group Project.) Design a survey to determine how much time women in your community spend in these three activities each week. Compile the results and compare them to the data in the table. Check your library to see if more current data is available from the United Nations. Why might or might not your community be typical of the United States today?

Application 43

World Army Sizes

Were the sizes of world armies smaller in 1991, when the Cold War was ending, than they had been four years previously in 1987? The following table supplies some information.

Country	Troops per 1,000 Population 1987	Troops per 1,000 Population 1991	Troop Levels (in thousands) 1987	Troop Levels (in thousands) 1991
Britain	5.8	5.2	328	301
France	10.0	9.5	559	542
Poland	11.7	8.0	441	305
Nigeria	1.3	0.8	138	94
Brazil	3.8	1.9	541	295
Argentina	3.8	2.2	118	70
Pakistan	6.1	6.8	645	803
India	1.9	1.4	1,502	1,200
China	3.3	2.8	3,530	3,200
Taiwan	18.5	20.5	365	424
South Korea	14.4	17.2	604	750
North Korea	41.3	55.0	838	1,200
United States	9.3	8.4	2,279	2,115

Source: U. S. Arms Control and Disarmament Agency.

1. Name two major countries that are not included in this table. Give any reasons that you can think of for not including them along with these countries.

2. Do you think larger armies or smaller armies would be associated with a safer world? Write a sentence or two giving your answer and reason.

3. We want to explore the following question: To what extent did the armies in these countries change in size from 1987 to 1991? Consider whether you want to focus on the variables giving troop levels, the variables giving the troop rate for each country's population, or both of these variables. You might also want to consider the percentage change in one of these variables from 1987 to 1991. Make at least two plots that display information concerning how the army sizes changed. You can use either one-variable or two-variable plots. Make sure you label both the United States and any other countries that stand out in the plots.

4. Using the information displayed in your plots and any additional numerical calculations you need, write a paragraph discussing to what extent the armies in these countries increased or decreased in size from 1987 to 1991. Include your reasons for choosing the variable or variables that you analyzed, and mention any especially interesting relationships you discovered.

Application 44

Who Was the Greatest Yankee Home Run Hitter?

The following table lists five of the greatest New York Yankees' home run hitters with the number of home runs each hit while a Yankee.

Babe Ruth		Lou Gehrig		Mickey Mantle		Roger Maris		Reggie Jackson	
Year	HR	Year	HR	Year	HR	Year	HR	Year	HR
1920	54	1923	1	1951	13	1960	39	1977	32
1921	59	1924	0	1952	23	1961	61	1978	27
1922	35	1925	20	1953	21	1962	33	1979	29
1923	41	1926	16	1954	27	1963	23	1980	41
1924	46	1927	47	1955	37	1964	26	1981	15
1925	25	1928	27	1956	52	1965	8		
1926	47	1929	35	1957	34	1966	13		
1927	60	1930	41	1958	42				
1928	54	1931	46	1959	31				
1929	46	1932	34	1960	40				
1930	49	1933	32	1961	54				
1931	46	1934	49	1962	30				
1932	41	1935	30	1963	15				
1833	34	1936	49	1964	35				
1934	22	1937	37	1965	19				
		1938	29	1966	23				
		1939	0	1967	22				
				1968	18				

1. Study these records. Which player appears to be the greatest home run hitter? Why did you choose this player?

2. Your task now is to rank the five players. You may wish to compute means, medians, or quartiles, or make line plots, stem-and-leaf plots, box plots, plots over time, or smoothed plots over time.

   How did you rank the five players? Describe your reasons and include your plots.

Women and Politics

The following table gives the year women received the right to vote and the percentage of seats held by women in the national legislative body for each of ten major countries in four different regions of the world.

Country	Year of Women's Right to Vote	Percentage of Seats Held by Women (1987)	Country	Year of Women's Right to Vote	Percentage of Seats Held by Women (1987)
Africa:			**Europe:**		
Angola	1975	14.5	East Germany	1919	32.2
Cameroon	1946	14.2	France	1944	6.4
Congo	1963	9.8	Italy	1945	12.9
Egypt	1956	3.9	Romania	1946	34.4
Kenya	1963	1.7	Spain	1931	6.4
Morocco	1963	0.0	Sweden	1921	28.5
Rwanda	1961	12.9	Switzerland	1971	14.0
Senegal	1945	11.7	USSR	1917	34.5
South Africa	1979	3.5	United Kingdom	1918	6.3
Zaire	1960	3.5	West Germany	1919	15.4
Asia and Pacific:			**North and South America:**		
Australia	1901	6.1	Argentina	1952	4.7
China	1949	21.2	Brazil	1934	5.3
India	1950	8.3	Canada	1918	9.6
Japan	1945	1.4	Costa Rica	1949	10.5
Malaysia	1957	5.1	Ecuador	1928	1.4
New Zealand	1893	14.4	Guatemala	1945	7.0
Pakistan	1947	8.9	Mexico	1953	10.8
Singapore	1948	3.8	Panama	1941	6.0
Thailand	1932	3.5	United States	1920	5.3
Viet Nam	1946	17.7	Venezuela	1947	3.9

Source: United Nations, *The World's Women 1970-1990.*

Questions of interest that relate to these data include the following:

Does there seem to be an overall association between the year that women received the right to vote and the percentage of legislative seats held by women as of 1987? That is, if women have had the vote in a country for a longer time, is the percentage of women legislators likely to be higher?

In terms of the two variables and these countries, what are the similarities and differences among these four regions of the world? That is, do some regions seem to have consistently larger percentages of women legislators than other regions? Did women generally obtain the right to vote earlier in some regions of the world than in other regions? Are there countries that are outliers, that seem to be different than the other countries in their region? If so, can you provide possible explanations?

How does the United States compare to the other countries in terms of these two measures of women's participation in politics?

The countries could also be grouped logically in a way that is different from geography—for example, grouping by predominant spoken language. Then the countries could be compared using this grouping.

1. Your task is to focus on a question such as one of the preceding. Construct at least two plots to explore answers to your question. Label interesting features on your plot. In a paragraph or two, state the question (or questions) you are investigating, describe what is shown by your plots, and summarize your results.

ACKNOWLEDGMENTS

Grateful acknowledgment is made to the following publishers, authors, and institutions for permission to use data from their publications.

p. 43: Best-selling children's books as of 1977. From *Eighty Years of Best Sellers* by A. P. Hackett and J. H. Burke. Copyright © 1977 by Reed Elsevier Inc. (pp. 43, 44). Reprinted with permission of R. R. Bowker, a Reed Reference Publishing Company.

p. 58: Top hits in 1959. From *The Billboard Book of Top 40 Hits,* by Joel Whitburn. Copyright © 1985 by Record Research.

p. 63: Number 1 hit records of 1966. From *The Billboard Book of Top 40 Hits,* by Joel Whitburn. Copyright © 1985 by Record Research.

p. 87: Number of occurrences of each letter. From *Student Math Notes,* copyright © 1983 by the National Council of Teachers of Mathematics.

p. 106: "Dual-Cassette Decks." Copyright 1993 by Consumers Union of U.S., Inc., Yonkers, NY 10703-1057. Adapted with permission from CONSUMER REPORTS BUYING GUIDE, 1993. Although this material originally appeared in CONSUMER REPORTS, the selective adaption and resulting conclusions presented are those of the author(s) and are not sanctioned or endorsed in any way by Consumers Union, the publisher of CONSUMER REPORTS.

p. 111: Early adolescent interests. From *The Journal of Early Adolescence,* vol. 1, No. 4, 1981, p. 369.

p. 115: Submarine sinkings. From *Beginning Statistics with Data Analysis,* by Mosteller, Fienberg, and Rourke. Copyright © 1983 by Addison-Wesley Publishing Company.

p. 124: Smoking vs. heart disease. From "Cigarette Smoking Related to Geographic Variations in Coronary Heart Disease Mortality and Expectation of Life in the Two Sexes," by Risteard Mulcahy, J. W. McGiluary, and Noel Hickey, in *American Journal of Public Health,* vol. 60, 1970.

p. 126: Animal gestation periods. Thanks to James Doherty, New York Zoological Society.

p. 135–6: Hits of the Beatles, Elvis, and The Supremes. From *The Billboard Book of Top 40 Hits,* by Joel Whitburn. Copyright © 1989 by Record Research.

p. 142: Tree age and diameter. From *Elements of Forest Mensuration,* 2d ed., by Chapman and Demeritt. Copyright © 1936 by Williams Press.

p. 173: High school sports injuries. From "Running in Pain," copyright © 1993, *New York Times.*